Great Women in the

Sport of Kings

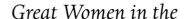

SPORTS AND ENTERTAINMENT
STEVEN A. RIESS, SERIES EDITOR

Great Women in the

Sport of Kings

MERICA'S TOP WOMEN JOCKEYS TELL THEIR STORIES

Edited by Scooter Toby Davidson and Valerie Anthony
Foreword by Sandy Schleiffers
Introduction by Mary Jo Festle

SU

Syracuse University Press

First Edition 1999
99 00 01 02 03 04   6 5 4 3 2 1

The paper used in this publication meets the minimum requirements of
American Standards for Information Sciences—Permanence of paper for Printed Library Material,
ANSI Z39.48-1984.♾

Great women in the sport of kings : America's top women jockeys tell their
stories / edited by Scooter Toby Davidson and Valerie Anthony ; foreword by
Sandy Schleiffers : introduction by Mary Jo Festle. —1st ed.
    p.   cm. — (Sports and entertainment)
    ISBN 0-8156-0565-X (cloth : alk. paper)
    1. Women jockeys—United States—Biography.   2. Jockeys—United
States—Biography. I. Davidson, Scooter Toby. II. Anthony, Valerie. III. Series.
SF336.A2G74 1999
798.4'0092—dc21
[B]   98-31881

Manufactured in the United States of America

To all those who have ever followed their hearts and said "yea" instead of "nay" to beat the odds stacked against them—and to all the horses who live to please us humans everyday

Scooter Toby Davidson. Originally from Miami, Florida but educated in New York City, Scooter spent more than twenty years designing and promoting various artistic concepts, including retail venues with Donald and Ivana Trump in the 1980s. The love of animals and a strong identification with the competitive nature of athletes sparked her interest in horseracing many years ago. Unable to ride horses herself because of a childhood accident, she wanted to find a way to honor women who do, hence, her contribution to this book.

Valerie Anthony. Born in England, Valerie hails from a journalistic family. Her father owned the *Weekly Sporting Review,* the largest sports paper in London for twenty-five years. She joined her father in the business and later founded the *Record Mirror,* a weekly show business publication still offered in England. In the 1960s Valerie came to New York, worked with artists and executives at RCA, and married Dee Anthony, who managed the careers of Tony Bennett, Peter Frampton, and Peter Allen. She also ran successful companies of her own. Currently, Valerie is coproducing projects with new artists and writers.

Contents

Foreword

*I*T IS ANOTHER BREEDER'S CUP DAY, a momentous day in horse racing. I find myself glued to the television, watching the first race. As the horses come out of the saddling paddock for the post parade, I start to think about how alive I felt when I came out to parade my mounts during this introduction of horse flesh to the betting crowd. When the horses approach the gate, adrenaline begins to course through my veins as I watch the handlers load the horses and hear someone shout, "One back," while the other handlers can be heard yelling, "Wait, no, no, no!" because some of the horses are acting up. In a fleeting instant there is a moment of silence, then the bell sounds, the gates swing back, and they're off. As I watch these beautiful animals and their riders jockey for position, my heart starts to pound, and my mind begins to remember the days of old when I rode these gallant animals to victory.

As I watch the second and then the fourth Breeder's Cup races, I note that a woman rider is aboard a mount in each. Julie Krone rides to a second-place victory in the second race, and Donna Barton finishes second as well in the fourth race. As I watch each of these races, I feel myself swell with pride for each woman jockey because she is living proof we made it in a male-dominated sport. I also feel some sadness because in my day of glory a chance to ride in such a prestigious race was not a reality, only a dream. A special kind of feeling consumes me as I watch Donna Barton perform and then listen to her synopsis of the race she has just ridden. I am just amazed at how much she looks like her mother, my dear friend, Patti Barton. I recall the experiences that Patti and I shared as we rode races together in 1969 and the early 1970s.

This was the dawn of a new age for women, in general, and in sport specifically. Although this was a volatile time, it was an exciting time because dreams and goals that stretched beyond the limitations of what a woman "should be" could now be sought and many times attained. It is fair, however, to say that those days were also days of turmoil and indecision for many women who possessed an overwhelming urge to be considered equals to their male counterparts but did not know where to start. Therefore, someone had to take a stand, and, thus, women like myself did so by refusing to be turned away from a profession that was termed gender specific because of tradition and the male ego.

It has been approximately thirty years since the first women conquered the barriers that prevented them from competing as equals with men in the sport of kings. Living proof of that "victory over tradition" is truly evident as Julie and Donna jockey their horses for second-place positions in the Breeder's Cup annals of time.

In 1969 I became the fourth woman jockey in American history to ride and win a race at a recognized Thoroughbred track, the first woman jockey to ride and win in a number of states, and the first woman jockey to be accepted into the Jockey's Guild. My racing career spanned some seven and one-half years during which I rode in races all over the United States, in Canada, and in Mexico. It was the best of times and sometimes the worst of times, but for all of that, I would not trade my racing career nor my part of history for anything.

Sandy Schleiffers

Dr. Schleiffers is the first woman ever to be admitted to the Jockey's Guild.

Preface

THOROUGHBRED HORSE RACING AND WOMEN ARE a combination not readily seen, written about, or even thought of in most parts of the world, America included. Thoroughbred horse racing, the "sport of kings" in history books and present-day media, was for centuries a highly male-dominated industry. But at last, the real "jewels in the crown," female jockeys, are making their presence known on the racetrack, in the winner's circle, and throughout society. Grabbing headlines and turning heads, they have used their skill, intelligence, sensitivity, and determination to establish themselves rightfully as a permanent presence alongside male counterparts, once the only gender "allowed" to be jockeys.

It has not been all that long since women were "granted" the right by the Thoroughbred racing industry to obtain a jockey's license. It was 1969, a liberating time in history for many people. Freedoms of all kinds were being sought. Maybe it was supportive and open-minded parents, immediate environments, the Beatles and the Rolling Stones, a shift in the vibrations of the universe, or a combination of the above, but we as authors of this book, living in the same time frame as the women who pioneered as jockeys, never had to endure the severities of the word *no* in our artistic vocations to the extent they did in their vocation, sports.

Why was it acceptable for women at that time to show their talents and earn their livings with paint on canvas, on recording disks, with cloth, needle, and thread, even on the ice skating rink but not as professionals on the backs of racing horses? As we discovered in our research, once the door was pried open for women to ride, it was quickly blown off its hinges, and one woman after another became gainfully employed with a good portion rising to fame within the industry and later achieving wider public acclaim.

As fans of horse racing over those years, we watched as more and more women's names appeared regularly as jockeys on the programs at the racetracks. Toward the late 1980s we noticed almost a whole new set of women riding and winning races at prestigious, larger racetracks. We started to follow their careers closely, keeping track of their accomplishments and collecting newspaper articles about them. No longer were they being portrayed as unfeminine wild rebels. When we went to racetracks for recreation and wagered on the horses they rode, we almost always collected tidy sums because they still were not being considered "sure bets" which increased the payoff prices at the betting windows.

We knew there was a story here, a story that needed to be shared with the world. We noticed that libraries and bookstores had books on how to wager at the racetrack, the history of horse racing, and, oh yes, one or two biographies of high-profile male jockeys of the past. In one remote library we found a highly editorialized book written back in 1973 on only some of the women who rode in the early 1970s, highlighting their antics more than their struggles and triumphs.

By 1995 all our creative thoughts solidified on how to present in book form the success, beauty, and devotion of the current women jockeys riding in America. As artists, we would paint their portraits with words and beautiful photos mostly from their own collections; we thought we would access the top women jockeys not only in standings at the racetracks but for life accomplishments as well. Visibility, attitude, perserverence, and diverse backgrounds and working conditions would also be determining factors. We would ask each one basically the same questions, things we wanted to know that presumably would be of interest to a larger audience; however, we would let them speak freely about any topic they wished because our interest in them as women, as people, went beyond their performances on the racetrack. "But will they talk to us?" we asked ourselves.

Each one of the jockeys honored our request to speak with her and to be part of this project. Each one was so gracious, so open. They invited us into their homes, introduced us to their family and friends. Whether it was in New York, Florida, or the Midwest, their receptions of us and of our ideas were equally warm and enthusiastic.

The result of our mutual admiration is evident in the pages of this book. Great women do come in small packages and we ourselves are still inspired everytime we reread their stories even though by now we know them by heart. We hope you feel the same way!

Scooter Toby Davidson
and Valerie Anthony

Acknowledgments

WE THANK AND ACKNOWLEDGE OUR LOVE for the following people who believed in the validity of this book.

Diane Nelson, Julie Krone, Paula Keim-Bruno, Jill Jellison, Gwen Jocson, Darci Rice, Rosemary Homeister, Jr., Donna Barton, Kristi Chapman, and Dodie Duys, are the current top female jockeys who inspired us to create this book. Once the project was underway they were most gracious and open with us, and we feel honored to have worked with them. Our thanks also go to Dr. Sandy Schleiffers and Patti Barton-Brown, who as two of the pioneer female jockeys in the sport gave us a "firsthand look at the past." How exciting and essential it was to have their contributions.

Nicole Catgenova at Syracuse University Press first of all understood the importance of publishing a book like this and, second, had the expertise, sensitivity, respect, and enthusiasm to allow us to honor these great women.

Cathy Dickinson used her talent to interpret and design the initial layout of the book when it was just a budding thought in the authors' minds and then spent countless hours on the computer.

The Muroff family, Melanie, Joanne, Renee, and Walter showed us at a formative age how to mix our love of horses with the excitement and competition of sports. Following the sport of horse racing became a solace through the years when everything else seemed to be going "haywire."

And we thank our mothers, who in life and now in their afterlives continue to give us unconditional love so we can go on and do great things.

Introduction

THOROUGHBRED HORSE RACING IS A SPORT WITH a long history and many traditions. The horses have always been at the heart of racing—always strong, fast specimens with their own unique personalities, carefully bred from centuries-long lines of excellence. They make possible the thrill of the race, the timeless magnet that draws the participants and spectators, but still remains new and unpredictable every day. Writing in 1857, representatives of the South Carolina Jockey Club described how a race course is much the same all over the world:

> The horses . . . paraded in the enclosure by the starting post, display, in their elastic step, the attributes of racers. Then follows the usual preparations: weighing the horses; rubbing down and saddling the horses; the expression of optimism in favor of one horse, and of doubts on the others; the mounting of the jockies [*sic*]; . . . the hum of anxiety as the word is given "to go"—and they are off; the diversified colors of the riders—purple, pink, green, scarlet . . . as they unfold their hues, and blazon, rainbow-like in the sun; the excitement of the populace as the coursers change places in the race, the interest increasing with every fresh struggle, till towards the close of the contest, the straining steeds enter the last quarter stretch, urged to their utmost speed and exertion, whips and spurs doing their work, and they near the distant post; the ground resounds beneath their rapid strides, the noise of their hoofs increases; the breathless moment of suspense is at hand; they are all together; it is any one's race; the earth trembles; they come; they fly by; they pass the post; the welkin rings with the delighted shouts of thousands, and all is over![1]

This description aptly fits the realities of racing not just in different places, but in different time periods. Indeed, while some particulars have changed, the essence of the sport remains unchanged—horse knowledge, racing rituals, and feelings of competition, joy, and disappointment have been passed down from generation to generation.

---

1. E. P. Milliken, et al., *The South Carolina Jockey Club* (Charleston, S.C.: Russell and Jones, 1957), 12.

Male dominance was just one of the traditions that persisted. Horse racing goes back to ancient times, during which the Romans brought the sport to Great Britain. The modern form of horse racing dates from 17th century England, where during the reigns of James I and Charles II, it gained its reputation as the "sport of kings." Owning and breeding horses was not profitable; in fact, it was quite a losing proposition. Therefore only royalty and nobility could afford the leisure and riches to patronize the sport. This elite did not race horses as a business, but as a recreational pastime. Horse races served a number of purposes: as a forum to test the skill of their breeds; as exciting contests affording the opportunity to wager (and demonstrate one's wealth); and as a social gathering for those of like breeding, wealth, and interest. This upper-class cohort developed both racing and its social rituals. Consistent with their role as patrons and their desire for deference, they often permitted people from lower classes to enjoy the races as spectators (as well as to care for the horses). The sport, then, had a long tradition of exclusiveness, most prominently with regard to social class (which was related to economic standing, race, ethnicity, and religion), but also with regard to the sex of its participants. On the other side of the Atlantic, American gentlemen imported horses and transplanted racing customs from their colonial rulers. They saw themselves as perpetuating a noble sport, and having a duty to hand down "unimpaired to their sons, and their sons' sons . . . the high character and enjoyments of . . . a rich legacy that has descended to them in trust from an honorable ancestry." They too saw horse racing as recreation, not business, and as a way to bring "social delight" to the gentry while permitting the "cheerful peasantry" to look on. Women, too, were onlookers, many of whom came, according to their menfolk, *to be seen,* as well as *to see.* Ladies could not belong to the Jockey Club; but they could "vie . . . with each other in the little coquetries every accomplished belle knows well how to avail herself of, to secure the devotion of some popular beau."[2]

Despite the persistence of many traditions, horse racing in the United States has undergone some significant changes over the years. After their successful revolution from Britain, Americans did not give up the sport, but did put their own distinctive mark on it. They came to regard horses as a symbol of their own aspirations and new identity: as free and independent; as having a practical role to play in building a strong agricultural republic; as individual animals who won or lost on the basis of their talents; and as capable of progress.[3] Not surprisingly, then, Americans stopped depending on British assistance and began breeding their own native stock of horses. American jockeys developed their own innovative style of riding,

2. Quoted in Milliken, et. al., *The South Carolina Jockey Club,* 210; see also Nancy L. Struna, "The Founding of Sport and the Formation of an Elite: The Chesapeake Gentry, 1650–1720s," *Journal of Sport History* 13, no. 3 (winter 1986), 212–20; and T. H. Breen, "The Cultural Significance of Gambling among the Gentry of Virginia," *William and Mary Quarterly* 34 (Apr. 1977), 239–57.

3. Nancy L. Struna, "The North-South Race: American Thoroughbred Racing in Transition, 1823–1850," *Journal of Sport History,* vol. 8, no. 2 (summer 1981), 51.

with their saddles forward and with shortened stirrups and reins. Owners adjusted the distance of races and started using dirt tracks; they began to race younger horses and use lighter jockeys. Jockeys themselves eventually came to be seen as professionals, not as private servants. Historic events certainly affected U.S. horse racing. The Civil War, for example, interrupted the sport's growth; urbanization changed the sport from a rural to an urban mass spectacle; a resurgence of racism around 1900 meant the exclusion of African American jockeys; reformers criticized the sport's corruption, successfully eliminating it from almost every state in the union; commercialism shifted the sport's emphasis from recreation to business and profit. The sport has adapted itself to all these changing circumstances. New circuits and rivalries developed. Leading authorities established the Jockey Club to control racing by licensing its participants. State commissions arose to regulate the now-prolific pari-mutuel betting. Finally, technological advances also altered the game, so that the starting gates are steel, horses wear aluminum shoes, and stewards can check videotape for fouls. The sport has changed over time to assure its continued survival.[4]

Women's role in society changed over time. In the mid-nineteenth century, women did not participate in sports. Victorian gender roles decreed that a woman should stay at home and be pious, pure, and submissive, not assertive and athletic. Activities like running, jumping, and horse *racing* (as opposed to horseback riding—a basic mode of transportation in the nineteenth century) were considered quite dangerous to a woman's frail constitution because the jarring might displace her pelvic organs and render her unable to have children. It was also believed that strenuous public competition could lead to a woman's nervous breakdown or arouse sexual feelings in participants or spectators that were thought to be inappropriate. Even if propriety had allowed it, practical matters such as a dress to the ground, multi-layered petticoat, suffocating corset, and sidesaddle would have made racing extremely difficult. Not surprisingly, Pierre de Coubertin, the founder of the modern Olympics, insisted that sports should be reserved as a showcase for male athleticism with "female applause as reward."[5]

As the twentieth century progressed, matters improved. Women were permitted to receive more education, work in new occupations, keep their own earnings, vote, wear less restrictive clothing, and limit the number of children they bore. They even were allowed to participate in some organized sports—within limits, of course. These were different, "feminized" games, usually segregated by sex. Often they were performed in private, as in intramurals at women's colleges, so that men would not see women be competitive and sweaty. Sometimes the rules were altered for female participants—as with 6-woman, half-court, two-dribble bas-

4. David Levinson and Karen Christensen, *Encyclopedia of World Sport: From Ancient Times to the Present,* vol. 2 (Santa Barbara, Calif.: ABC-CLIO, 1996), 443–44.

5. Pierre de Coubertin quoted in Janet Woolum, *Outstanding Women Athletes: Who They Are and How They Influenced Sports in America* (Phoenix, Ariz.: The Oryx Press, 1992), 33; Victoria Sherrow, *Encyclopedia of Women and Sports* (Santa Barbara, Calif.: ABC-CLIO, 1996), ix–xv.

ketball—so women wouldn't overexert themselves.[6] While they played, women were encouraged to stress cooperation as much as competition, and after the contest they would gather with
their opponents for tea and cookies. Athletes also began displaying "apologetic behavior"—
actions intended to minimize "unfeminine" aspects of sports or to highlight the "feminine"
apsect. Examples of apologetic behavior included wearing pink ribbons or frilly uniforms, assur-
ing interviewers that they had boyfriends and wanted to have children, or emphasizing the rel-
ative unimportance of the game to their lives. "We travel and love to play basketball," said U.S.
team member Margaret Holloran in 1958. "We don't want to play forever, however. Like everybody else, we want to get married."[7] Male athletes did not need to behave in such a way, because
sports were considered consistent with and complementary to the masculine gender role.
Women's apologetic behavior, then, was an adaptation to the notion that sports were "unfeminine," which in the popular mind meant "masculine," which in turn could also connote "les-
bian." By speaking or behaving in apologetic ways, female athletes tried to compensate for the
unfeminine reputation of their sport, to counterbalance the disapproval they encountered. In
effect, women athletes conveyed the message that although they wanted to be athletes, they
also wanted to be accepted as normal, feminine women.

Despite these extra burdens on female athletes, women in the first half of the twentieth century were grateful. Now they could begin to enjoy some competitive athletic opportunities, and this applied to equestrian sports as well. A few prominent women owned
thoroughbreds early in the century: Mary Hirch was licensed as a trainer in 1935; four women
qualified for individual dressage competition in the 1952 Olympics; "Grandma" Neva Burright
achieved great popularity and world records in harness racing in the 1950s.[8] But still, despite the
fact that women seemed to ride and love horses in at least the same proportion as men, and
despite the fact that their smaller size made them naturally well suited to be jockeys, all licensed
flat track jockeys were male.[9]

During the 1960s, however, the United States witnessed not one, but two, of the most
significant social transformations of its history. The black civil rights movement and the
women's liberation movement were attempting to gain for their disadvantaged constituents

6. Susan K. Cahn, *Coming on Strong; Gender and Sexuality in Twentieth-Century Women's Sport* (Cambridge, Mass.:
Harvard Univ. Press, 1994), 4–5.
7. Mary Jo Festle, *Playing Nice: Politics and Apologies in Women's Sports* (New York: Columbia Univ. Press, 1996), 48.
8. "Women Take No Back Seat in Sulky," *New York Times*, Jan. 26, 1969, sec. 5, p. 3; the Olympics formally opened
the door to female participation in dressage, endurance, and show jumping in 1912, although no woman actually
qualified for the events until 1952. American women competed in the Olympic equestrian events in 1964.
9. Over the years, there had been many instances of informal racing by women, and some evidence of formal races,
such as exhibitions and "powder puff" derbies. These were occasional, and sometimes considered sideshows; however
talented, the women involved were not officially licensed by racing authorities. See, for example, the Dorothy Tyler
entry in Sherrows, *Encyclopedia of Women and Sports*; Nancy L. Struna, "Gender and Sporting Practice in Early America, 1750–1810" *Journal of Sport History* 18, no. 1 (spring 1991), 24–27; and "Eleven Jockeys Fined," *New York Times*, Jan. 17,
1969, p. 21.

increased power, respect for their capabilities, and equal opportunities. Borrowing ideas and techniques from the African American struggle, women began asking for an end to discrimination in corporations, schools, banks, the health professions, police departments, churches, families, the media, and peoples' minds. In the face of lawsuits, demonstrations, lobbying, consciousness-raising, and constant insistence on women's rights, barriers came tumbling down. Laws, institutions, and attitudes all changed, and women increasingly entered male-dominated fields, becoming lawyers, doctors, professors, judges, politicians, ministers, journalists, soldiers, fire fighters, construction workers, and technicians. Sports, long a male preserve, were not immune to the transformation. Between 1965 and 1975, females gained entry into Little League baseball, the Boston Marathon, and the Indianapolis 500. Professional women tennis players won purses equal to those of men at the U.S. Open; women umpires earned the right to arbitrate women's games; women journalists gained the right to interview male football players; and intercollegiate athletes achieved equal athletic scholarships, decent uniforms, better coaching, and more contests. A stunned world watched in amazement as women reversed years of discouragement and seized new opportunities to demonstrate exactly how capable they were. Serious and talented athletes got chances to become champions, and average women, who started jogging, joining gyms, and taking up tennis, began taking their health and fitness seriously.

But these pioneers in the athletic revolution faced some serious difficulties. Kathy Switzer was chased off the course by a male official while trying to run the Boston Marathon. Little girls were kicked off teams as parents and lawyers fought over their right to participate in ball games. Told that they deserved just ten to twenty-five percent of the purse at mixed tournaments, women tennis pros had to start their own separate women-only tour to win larger purses. Pro basketball players endured poor practice facilities, insect-ridden lockers, crowded hotel rooms, stalled buses, and high school-like budgets. Some male team owners insisted their female players attend charm school and play exhibitions against Playboy bunnies. At colleges and universities, women's sports received about two percent of athletic budgets in the early 1970s. Female coaches and administrators lived in fear of losing their reputations and jobs as stories circulated of colleagues being fired or "labeled" lesbians after they pushed for equal resources.

Early female athletes had difficulty being taken seriously. Bobby Riggs, who became famous for his "Battle of the Sexes" challenge match against Billie Jean King in 1973, believed women tennis pros played only 25 percent as well as men, and declared, "Women's place is in the bedroom and the kitchen, in that order."[10] When covering women's athletic events, even sympathetic sportswriters constantly reminded readers that these athletes were different, in part by repeatedly referring to their looks. In a story about Chris Evert's play at the U.S. Open, for example, a reporter spent paragraphs describing her jewelry, long pink fingernails, tanned skin, dark eyelashes, and lack of sweat.[11]

10. Festle, *Playing Nice,* 158.
11. Ibid., 154.

In this context, horse racing witnessed its own revolution. A handful of pioneering women, such as Kathy Kusner, Penny Ann Early, Diane Crump, Barbara Jo Rubin, and Tuesdee Testa, were all simultaneously trying to gain a foothold as jockeys. But many racing authorities simply held sexist views. "They're not strong enough to be good riders. They'll freeze. They'll panic," insisted Nick Jemas, managing director of the Jockey Club. He believed they did not have the lightening reflexes necessary to make instantaneous adjustments, would endanger male jockeys with poor decisions, and could not physically handle the inevitable accidents. "This is no game for girls," he concluded.[12] Throughout 1968 and 1969, state racing commissions repeatedly found excuses not to license women: it would be too expensive to find separate dressing quarters for female jockeys; the language of their bylaws said jockeys were to be male (and these bylaws would have to be painstakingly reconsidered); the particular women who applied were amateur, or too inexperienced, too unskilled, too old, or too young; male jockeys were too gentlemanly to compete against women.[13] Knowing their ability as gallopers and exercisers, a few trainers wanted to give them a chance, but they hesitated in the face of opposition from male jockeys. So the female hopefuls used a variety of methods, including networking with the right people, working their way up, and suing (or threatening to sue) under the nondiscrimination in employment clause of the Civil Rights Act of 1964. All of these women benefited from a combination of hard work, patience, talent, self-confidence, luck, and assistance from people who believed in them. Mostly, though, it was their own determination that achieved change. Kathy Kusner reapplied month after month and finally appealed to the courts before she obtained her jockey's license from the state of Maryland. Unfortunately, due to injury, she was not the first woman to compete against men on the flat track. Florida changed its rules instead and Diane Crump got that honor on February 7, 1969, riding Bridle 'N Bit at Hialeah Park in Miami. Although she finished tenth out of twelve, the dam had cracked. Barbara Jo Rubin and Tuesdee Testa quickly followed in Crump's footsteps, and, inspired by their feat, even more did the same.

Like all trailblazers, these women encountered some difficulties. Once they were legally permitted to race, female jockeys met with boos and skepticism from spectators. "I'd never bet on a race with a girl jockey," explained one bettor. "The male jockeys just wouldn't be able to ride my horse without thinking of protecting the girl."[14] When they lost, they heard gendered taunts such as, "Go home and do the dishes." Resentment from male jockeys manifested itself in cool treatment and lack of inclusion, but other times it was more organized and active. At Churchill Downs and Hialeah, male jockeys boycotted races that Penny Ann Early and Barbara

12. Steve Cady, "Jemas Insist Girl Jockeys Are Just a Passing Fancy," *New York Times,* Feb. 16, 1969, sec. 5, p. 8.

13. "Kathy Krusner Faces New Hurdle," *New York Times,* Nov. 23, 1967, 64; "Kathy Kusner's Dream 'Scratched,'" *New York Times,* Feb. 9, 1968, p. 60; "Miss Kusner Loses Again in Bid for Jockey Licence," *New York Times,* Apr. 28, 1968, sec. 5, p. 8; "Woman Jockey Puts Off Debut," *New York Times,* Nov. 17, 1968, sec. 5, p. 10; "Jockey's Aid Warns of Hazards to Women," *New York Times,* Nov. 27, 1968, p. 58.

14. Steve Cady, "Girl Jockeys Are Invading the Big A," *New York Times,* Mar. 11, 1969, p. 52.

Jo Rubin were scheduled to ride in.[15] Sometimes male jockeys harassed the women verbally, or committed fouls intended to scare their mounts. Others tried to injure or intimidate the riders: once someone threw a rock into the trailer Rubin was using as a dressing area; in the middle of a race, other women felt the sting of a whip on the face or neck. "You'd hear whispering in the corner: 'Let's get the girl,'" admitted Angel Cordero.[16]

Like other pioneering female athletes, jockeys also had difficulty winning respect. They were not always taken seriously. Skeptics said they would not have the determination to stick with it. Indeed Nick Jemas predicted female jockeys would be a temporary fad, like the hula hoop.[17] Uncertain of how to deal with this sports "novelty," sportswriters routinely mentioned women jockey's hair length and eye color and post-race attire in their stories, which they never did when discussing male jockeys. Even the *New York Times* referred to Penny Ann Early as "the country's shapeliest jockey."[18] At press conferences, female jockeys were asked irrelevant questions, such as, "Do you have plans for getting married?" which constantly reminded them that they were doing something unusual. Barbara Rubin was asked, "Do you feel this endangers your femininity?" She answered, "When you're out there riding your ride to win, you're a jockey. Afterwards, I'm a lady." Her careful answer illustrated the fine line female athletes walked: they didn't want to act too tough because then they'd be seen as "masculine" and disapproved of; on the other hand, if they behaved too apologetically and "too feminine," they risked not being taken seriously as jockeys. So some acted just like male jockeys (including taking part in fist fights when threatened). Others adopted an extra-feminine strategy, such as asking for a kiss from the owner after a win, or joking about their flowered underwear. When she said, "Next to horse racing, men are my favorite hobby," Penny Ann Early managed to both highlight her heterosexuality and suggest racing was just an unimportant "hobby" in the same apologetic fashion female athletes had done for decades.[19]

The pressure on the first generation of jockeys was intense. They felt that they had to be perfect and that any mistake they made would be fatal—not only to themselves but to other and future women jockeys. They believed, with good reason, that to be considered effective jockeys they had to perform not equal to but *better than* male jockeys. And it was a no-win situation. If they got good mounts, critics said it was because owners wanted them solely for publicity (which some did). If they won races, skeptics attributed it to male jockeys holding back,

15. At Hialeah, the male jockeys dropped their boycott after a day—after they were fined. "Woman Jockey Puts Off Debut," *New York Times,* Nov. 17, 1968, p. 25; "Jockey Boycott Prevents Barbara Rubin From Riding at Tropical," *New York Times,* Jan. 16, 1968, p. 49.

16. J. E. Vader, "Riding High," *Ms.,* June 1988, 30

17. Jemas, quoted in Vader, "Riding High," 30

18. Quoted in Lynn Haney, *The Lady Is a Jock* (New York: Dodd, Mead, and Company, 1973), 11, 17. See also "2 Women Jockeys Get First Victories," *New York Times,* Mar. 2, 1969, sec. 5, pp. 1, 23. Sometimes papers also prefaced their names with "Mrs." Male jockeys were not referred to by any title.

19. Haney, *The Lady Is a Jock,* 11, 17.

or said the women were on such heavily-favored horses that they could not lose. If they did lose, it "proved" that they were not capable.[20] This made it almost impossible for female jockeys to gain legitimacy. Every jockey had her own horror stories, but perhaps the greatest problem of all was the doubt or disinterest from many owners and trainers—without whom there would never be an opportunity to prove themselves.

But when given the chance, these jockeys did prove themselves. Four years before Billie Jean King defeated Bobby Riggs in their well-publicized "Battle of the Sexes," nineteen-year-old Barbara Jo Rubin became the first female jockey in the United States to win in a regular pari-mutuel flat race against male jockeys. She did so before a record crowd at Charles Town race track on February 22, 1969 on a colt named Cohesion. Victories by Tuesdee Testa in California and Diane Crump in Florida followed just a week or so later. Gradually there were other significant "firsts"—first woman to ride at each track around the country, first to gain 100 victories (Mary Bacon, June 1971), first to ride in the Kentucky Derby (Diane Crump, May 1970), first to be admitted to the Jockey's Guild (Sandy Schleiffers, 1970), first to win a stakes race (Robyn Smith, March 1973). Some of the "chill" began to thaw. Indeed, after her first victory at Aqueduct, Rubin experienced the same initiation ritual as male apprentices when they won their first race there: being doused with a pail of water.[21] Though her career was cut short by injuries, Rubin's winning percentage (she won 22 out of the 89 races she rode in) made an impression. People did not quickly forget that the new jockeys were female, nor did all the hurdles instantly fall, but at least in addition to the resentment, ridicule, and skepticism now came positive publicity, fan letters, more opportunities, and support from some jockeys, trainers, owners, and spectators. The initial spotlight of publicity dimmed, and they were left to the same career difficulties as other jockeys: practicing, traveling, making weight, winning, losing, and above all, hustling mounts.

Even though they have shared the same qualities and experiences as other women athletes, in some ways women jockeys have been the "forgotten athletes." As a group, jockeys are often underappreciated as athletes, in part because the horse does so much work and is seen as the primary performer.[22] But like all elite athletes, female jockeys are very talented physically. They must have legs as strong as soccer players, hands with the firm control yet soft touch of golfers, and the balance and flexibility of gymnasts. They are coordinated, have quick reflexes, and must be in great physical condition to have the endurance necessary to push a tiring horse the final eighth of a mile. They have an excellent sense of timing. Like all fine athletes, jockeys are extremely competitive, self-motivated and self-disciplined, and possess an astounding abil-

20. Steve Cady, "Girl Jockeys Are at the Big Apple to Stay; for a While at Least," *New York Times,* Mar. 16, 1969, sec. 5, p. 10.
21. Joe Nichols, "Miss Rubin Guides Bravy Galaxy, $28.20, to Victory in Debut at Aqueduct," *New York Times,* Mar. 15, 1969, p. 39.
22. For a report about the excellent physical condition of jockeys as "forgotten athletes," see Jay Posner, "Reining Athletes: Jockeys Stand up with the Best," *San Diego Union Tribune,* Aug. 23, 1995, p. D1.

ity to concentrate and focus on their performance. In order to succeed, they must be totally dedicated to their sport. That means they must work consistently hard practicing their craft, for long hours. They must take great care of their bodies, which means closely watching their intake of food, drink, and vitamins, being sure they get enough rest, and sacrificing a normal social life. They also share the mental and psychological attributes of champions, including tactical savvy and a cool head in the face of heated competition. Courageous with their bodies, fearlessly risking injury, they dedicate their hearts as well, going all out and risking defeat. They must be mentally tough enough to cope with both failure and success.

Although there are similarities in both in their dilemmas and in the ways they respond to them, female jockeys are also different from other female athletics. Their sport is unique. Depending so heavily on the horse's performance, it is neither exactly an individual sport nor is it a team sport. Racing on top of and alongside thousand-pound animals speeding at thirty-five miles an hour is hazardous. Inevitably, jockeys take terrible falls, and sometimes they get trampled as horses pass. Julie Krone, for example, has broken her back, shattered her ankle, punctured her elbow, fractured her two hands, and bruised her heart. Finally, horse racing is one of those rare instances where men and women compete directly against one another. The characteristics needed by jockeys—including small size, balance, strength, the ability to communicate, racing savvy, and courage—make horse racing a sport where it's as possible for female athletes to excel as it is for male athletes.

Although horse racing traditionally was male-dominated, fortunately for women it does not seem to have had such a violent anti-female streak as sports like football and ice hockey. [23] Racing did not exactly welcome female jockeys (or trainers) with open arms, and it still does not have the percentage of women that it logically should. But racing has changed dramatically, and without as much of the ugliness as some institutions. The sexism that remains is more subtle; it is difficult to prove, though widely perceived.[24] Rather than exploding openly, the extant sexism bubbles quietly underneath the surface.

Women are obviously physically capable of and suited to the job. The evidence is clear: jockeys from Barbara Rubin to Julie Krone to Donna Barton have won. They have convinced skeptics. Even Nick Jemas, who so vehemently asserted women's inferiority in the early days, came to see things differently. "Times change and people change and the resentment faded, little by little," he explained in 1988. "Only a damn fool wouldn't change his mind."[25] Popular lit-

23. Mariah Burton Nelson, *The Stronger Women Get, the More Men Love Football: Sexism and the American Culture of Sports* (New York: Harcourt Brace, 1994).
24. See quotes or examples in Rick Teverbaugh, "Riding for Acceptance," *Anderson (Ind.) Herald-Bulletin,* Nov. 4, 1997; Suzy Mulligan, "Female Jockeys, Trainers Gaining a Strong Foothold," *Indianapolis Star,* Sept. 1, 1995; Mary Rampelinni, "Winning a Place," *Fort Worth Star-Telegram,* June 6, 1995; Dan Johnson, "Warhol Set to Ride 1000th Winner," *Des Moines Register,* June 24, 1993; Steve Bisheff, "Jenine Sahadi Trains Herself to Buck Odds," *Orange County Register,* Mar. 22, 1995.
25. Quoted in J. E. Vader, "Riding High," *Ms.* June 1988, 28–30.

erature and individual histories are replete with stories of an almost mystical bond between girls and their horses. In fact, some observers have begun stressing women's relationship and communication with horses as a reason why they are as good as, or better than, male jockeys.

Though unusual in the wider sports world, female and male jockeys competing against one another is no longer a novelty in horse racing. Although it is not yet clear whether there is a glass ceiling holding them back, neither are female jockeys mere tokens. Their presence is taken for granted at tracks, especially in certain parts of the nation, and sex is no longer one of the pressing issues in horse racing.

The women featured in this book belong to a second generation of female jockeys. They are not pioneers, but are grateful to have had the opportunity to build upon their foundation. Despite having had many barriers cleared for them, they are significant in their own right. Although fairly commonplace at every track, women still constitute a small minority of jockeys. These women are unusual in their ability, too. Some of them have great prospects ahead, and many have already proven a high level of success. They represent 1,000 victory winners, riders at the Breeder's Cup, winners of Triple Crown events, and the recipient of an Eclipse Award. Many jockeys ride, but few manage to stand out and excel over the long haul as these women have. The competition is fierce, and the lifestyle difficult. As Donna Barton says, riders might make it look smooth, but "there's nothing easy about it." Scooter Davidson and Valerie Anthony have done a nice job of interviewing these jockeys, providing readers with a glimpse into the texture of their lives. As interviewers, they consistently asked each rider certain questions, so that all the jockeys address growing up, how they got started in the saddle, and special moments and difficulties in their careers. They talk about their role models and their favorite horses. They relate what it's like to be a *female* jockey, and what it's like to have fans. They reflect upon their social lives and their hopes for the future. In some of their most telling answers, they reveal what they would say to a young girl who wanted to be a jockey.

Each woman's story is unique, but certain common themes do emerge. With regard to women's capabilities, all are unanimous that females have the strength necessary to win, and that there are many characteristics as important to winning as muscles. Although they certainly do not deny sexism exists in horse racing, and some relate specific incidents they've experienced, as a group they tend to downplay sexism. There are many possible explanations for this outlook: they "made it" without encountering too much prejudice; they overcame discrimination by ignoring it and would like others to do the same; they don't want to be perceived as complainers (like many women in the postfeminist 1990s); or things are so much better than they used to be that the remaining prejudice seems insignificant. Regardless of the reason, it is clear that like other female athletes, these women want to be seen as athletes, not *female* athletes. They are tired of qualifiers reminding them that they are unusual, and they want to be judged on their merits. As Julie Krone said, "I don't want to be just the best female jockey in the world.

I want to be the best jockey." At the same time, their concern for girls' and women's sports also shines through clearly. They speak glowingly of female role models, support one another in the locker room, and provide thoughtful, heartfelt messages to girls who might be future jockeys.

What also comes through in each of these women's stories is their dedication to their sport. Their social lives—to the degree that social lives are possible with such a grueling schedule—revolve around people in horse racing, who are their "family." Their routine acceptance of injury and dismissal of fear illustrate not only their courage, but their passion for the sport. They love not just the excitement and competition of racing, but also the horses at the heart of it. That passion lured a number of these women away from other careers, and it spurs most to say that they hope to continue in a horse-related career after they no longer can be jockeys. Their lives and identities are almost wholly subsumed in racing, and they do not see this as a sacrifice.

This collection of interviews with successful contemporary jockeys constitutes important work. It presents these women's experiences and attitudes, not as filtered by others, but in their own words, so that the reader can "hear" their voices. It is valuable to those interested in the history of Thoroughbred horse racing in the United States and to those interested in the history and current status of women and female athletes. It is a must-read for people who love horse racing and who admire the exceptional athletes who partner with the horses to make it the exciting sport it is.

Mary Jo Festle
Author of Playing Nice: Politics and Apologies in Women's Sports

Great Women in the
Sport of Kings

Diane Nelson. *Courtesy of Jim Lampson.*

Diane Nelson

Growing up on Long Island, New York, Diane knew at a very early age that she wanted a life with horses. As a teenager she was tall, 5'6" at age sixteen, and pretty enough to be a Hollywood starlet but was happy just working with horses on the farm. At the time she was not thinking "jockey," but she was not thinking college either. Encouraged by family and coworkers, she made her way up to New England in 1986 and hit her stride at Rockingham Park Racetrack, capturing four riding titles. She was the leading rider there at just age twenty.

Riding on the New York Thoroughbred circuit was and still is Diane's career goal. She has maintained her status as a regular rider for top trainers there for more than ten years, quite an accomplishment because the Northeast is the most competitive market in the country. Trainers hire her because she is a strong rider with a light touch and is mentally very sharp. With numerous wins, titles, and faithful employers she has shown the world that a woman does not have to compromise her feminitity, values, and vocational desires to fit into an industry that has been predominatly male for hundreds of years.

The Beginning

"I want a pony! I want a pony" I pleaded with my parents ever since I could remember. I grew up in Holtzville on Long Island, New York. We had horses on our property when I was five years old, but my parents got rid of them by the time I was seven because they went into the plant nursery business and needed room on the land for their inventory. I kept bugging my parents, "I want a horse, a pony . . . please!" My older sister rode when my parents still had a lot of property that they weren't using for business. I had three much older brothers and sisters. There were six kids total in my family. My parents gave away the horses when they became a problem by eating and rolling on the plants around the same time that my sister, ten years senior, stopped riding. So when people ask me, "Did you grow up with horses?" I have to say not really because by the time I was old enough to ride, there weren't any left on my parents' land.

I did everything to persuade my mother to get me a horse, including making up schedules of how and when I would feed him and take care of him and where he would sleep. I was relentless. So, finally, when my mother thought I was old enough, three years or so after my very formal proposals, she took me over to a friend's house who had a daughter my age. They had horses.

The daughter and I hit it off and we became best friends. I was in heaven. I was ten years old when I first rode a horse. I spent afternoons and all my summers there. It was like a real farm to me because there were not only horses but donkeys, cats, dogs, and other animals. They were really great people; I have great memories of every moment there. On school days I took the bus in the afternoon directly to their house so my mother didn't have to bother taking me over each day. My three older brothers and sisters were all in college by then, and my next oldest brother and sister (I'm the baby in the family) had no interest in horses whatsoever. My mother always liked horses but was very busy with the nursery plant business all the time. My older sister, who used to ride a lot, went into the navy, so I was the only active horse lover in the house at that time.

The Transition

I remember my mother asking me periodically during my high school years, "So what do you want to do? Where do you want to go to college?" All I could ever answer was, "I want to do something with horses." I helped my mother and father with their business in those years in addition to riding at my friend's house everyday after school. After a time, my parents said to me, "Well, we will send you to a college in New England where there is accessibility to horses." I thought to myself, "But I just really want to work with horses." I couldn't imagine any other career; I couldn't even think "college."

No college. I started to work in stables. I went from one job to another, but that is how I met people. I cleaned horse stalls at a barn a couple of days a week in high school. I got a job on a horse breeding farm in the summer of eleventh grade. I loved that job. Actually, I remember I had a job in between those, breaking in two-year-old horses in Florida when I was fifteen. I was offered the job at Christmastime because the spring is when owners and trainers first break in horses. I had to talk my reluctant mother into letting me because it meant leaving school for the semester and making up time and credits in the summer. This job was a dream come true, I thought, and I was amazed that I was trusted to do this job when I was just fifteen years old.

I think it was at this point that my parents realized how much horses and a life with horses meant to me. I did come back in the summer, made up the school work, and worked on the breeding farm as well. I really felt so lucky all these opportunities were coming up. It was magical; I wished for things and they would happen. Nowadays when kids come up to me in the New York area and ask about working with horses, I tell them, "Well, you will probably have to go down to Florida or the Carolinas to get the experience of breaking in horses like I did because that is where the opportunities are." I really feel strongly about my experiences there.

By the start of twelfth grade my parents became totally supportive of my desire to work with horses. Then another opportunity came at the breeding farm at which I was working. It sounded so crazy at the time, but the stud manager came up to me at the end of the breeding season and asked me if I would like to go to New Zealand. He was from New Zealand. He said their breeding season was just starting over there because they were in the Southern Hemisphere. All I wanted to do was to keep learning, so again, I had to go home and beg my parents to let me go. I explained to them that to fly me over there would be the same expense as a semester of college tuition. They thought it over and agreed.

I went to New Zealand. At first I wasn't making much money, only seventy dollars every two weeks, so I got another job galloping horses at a Thoroughbred training center. I learned so much there. At that point I still wasn't thinking "jockey." I was so happy just to be working with horses. I didn't entertain the thought of being a jockey because I thought I was too big—5'6" when I was sixteen years old. I was skinny, but everyone said to me, "Oh you'll fill out by the time you're eighteen." Well, I'm thirty-one now, still waiting to fill out!

When I was younger, before my horse-caring jobs, I stood with my friends by the pool and said, "I wish I was short with little tiny feet." In my subconscious I guess I always thought I was too big. Now I know why I used to say that to my friends; there was a reason behind that thinking!

New Zealand was great. The culture, the job, and the people were wonderful over there. It was just as interesting for the people to have me there as it was for me to be there. I was there for six months, and then my parents came over and we traveled the country for another month. It was fantastic, and I was finally earning a living with horses. A big change was happening in my life. My mother used to say when I was little, "It costs money to ride horses," so I was thrilled just to be able to be around horses, to ride them, and to earn a living with them at this point. Wow, someone was actually paying me to ride horses; I couldn't believe it.

I realized there were so many avenues at that time (the early eighties) that I could follow for jobs in the horse industry. There was office work such as charting the bloodlines of horses for

A job in the horse industry felt certain in my future.
Courtesy of the Nelson family

Diane Nelson

breeding. There was physical work exercising and galloping horses in the morning and assistant trainer jobs opening up. The Thoroughbred horse industry was booming, and I felt certain I would always have a job in some capacity.

The Turning Point

When I came back to the United States, I went to Florida, all expenses paid plus a salary in tow, to another breeding farm owned by the Entenmann family. After I worked down there for a little while, they sent me with some horses to Monmouth Park, my first racetrack experience. The manager at the breeding farm, Robert, kept saying to me, "You should be a jockey, you know." I still thought that I was too tall, too big. I said to myself, "Well, I'll just be a gallop rider." But I never got heavy, never filled out as people said I would. I was eighteen years old by then, and I stayed light.

By the time I was nineteen romance had blossomed between Robert and me, and we married when I was twenty. He wanted to be a horse trainer and was very supportive of me becoming a jockey after seeing me exercise and gallop the horses. I guess I just needed to hear someone say the words, "You really should be a jockey. You can do it." I said, "Okay, I'll try it."

So as husband and wife we went from Monmouth Park in New Jersey to New York with some really nice horses. We both wound up working for a good trainer, Dominick Imperio, who gave me my first chance as a jockey. I used to gallop horses for him in the morning over at Belmont, and just as horses need to be "okayed" to start from the gate at a racetrack, so do apprentice jockeys. Dominick sent me to the gate with all the baby horses, the two year olds, so we could both get experience breaking from the starting gate. He let me ride my first race ever at Aqueduct Racetrack in 1986.

By now everyone was supportive of my decision to be a jockey. In fact, I recall that when I was still on the farm in Florida, I called my mother with the news that I was going to try to be a jockey, and I was really surprised how excited she was. It was at that point I realized how much she had always loved horses and that being a jockey was something she would have liked to do as well. I was expecting her to say, "Oh that's crazy. You should do something else; you're too big." She was very proud, actually, and said, "Really? How wonderful!" My father was supportive also, but he was worried about me getting hurt. Yet he was the kind of man who would never hold me back from something I sincerely wanted to do.

I rode two races that winter for Dominick at Aqueduct but found the New York circuit too hard for me to compete in the first time out, so we went up to New England. We spent the summer up at Rockingham Park in New Hampshire. My career really took off up there. I got a lot of work riding as a jockey. In fact, I was the leading rider two years in a row. My husband and I found ourselves in a new place with two new careers. We worked hard and were living our dream. We were "green" but had great opportunities and stayed north while most of the bigger trainers brought horses south. We had tons of work. The cold weather didn't bother us. It got to the point where I

4

was riding in every race every day. I loved it! I was so tired, but a "good" tired, every night. It was the time when *Dynasty* was on television, and I remember that I couldn't keep my eyes open through the show. By 9:00 P.M. I was out like a light.

We thought we had landed in heaven; it was beautiful living up in New England. We would go skiing on our days off, and I was so thrilled to be riding horses for a living and making good money at it.

Then I got hurt. My horse fell, and I fractured two vertebrae. I was laid up for three months and mad about it! I was leading rider at the time at Rockingham Park. My family was scared because I broke my back, but I had no spinal injury. As soon as I was able, I came back to work and was again leading rider.

I achieved so much up there: fastest time on such and such a horse, breaking track records for certain handicap races, "best" titles all over the place. I began to feel at this point that I was defending my "title," and I was there for the love of it. I knew it was time to move on. It was the same as going from junior high to high school.

I went to New Jersey. It was very emotional to leave New Hampshire; we had created a life there. A couple of good trainers that I had been riding for up there also decided at the same time to make the move to New Jersey with their horses. Again I was lucky because they knew me and knew my work, so I was able to get some starting work in yet another new and larger circuit. It was still a difficult adjustment to go from riding the best horses in the best races with everyone wanting me on their horses for two and one-half years to being a "no-one" in a different state. But once I got there it didn't matter because I was dazzled by the Meadowlands and all I cared about was that I was riding and making a living. My goal at the time was to have success in New Jersey but ultimately to return to New York. Some jockeys will say their goal is to ride in the Derby, but for me it was to return to ride in New York.

My husband and I split up at the same time. We went our separate ways in 1988–89. I returned to New York with huge successes on one horse in the winter of 1989. The horse kept winning and winning with me on it and kept going up in the ranks. I stayed on him, and he won stakes races. This brought me a lot of publicity. When something like that happens, it makes the rider a winner as well, and people start to take notice and other good horses become available.

I also went back the following summer to Monmouth Park to ride. I was going through my divorce at the time, and even though I did okay, as I look back I see how my emotions unfocused me as an athlete. I know today that even though I think certain distractions in my personal life are not going to affect me, they do. It is so important for an athlete to be mentally sharp. I've noticed through the years that a lot of jockeys, both male and female, who didn't make it in the industry couldn't deal with the mental and emotional stress issues; it wasn't that they were incompetent physically as athletes.

There is a lot of rejection in the business; I had to learn not to take it personally. A trainer might suddenly put another jockey on a horse that I had ridden to success countless times before.

Diane Nelson

This change could be for so many reasons, for instance, weight allowance. It's a business, and I had to realize it's nothing personal because the next race out I could be back on as the conditions changed.

I tell my agent, "Being a jockey is the only job I can keep getting fired from and still have the same job." Every time I don't get to ride a horse twice in succession I say, "Well, I got fired again!" But then I am hired again; I still have a job. I've learned to handle it mentally.

Many people think that there aren't many female jockeys because they can't handle the stress, but by ratio there are just as many males who have crumbled. It's not just a woman thing; many of the male jockeys who didn't make it come up to me years later and ask, "How do you deal with it? I couldn't."

I don't think specific trainers or owners are pro-women. I do think that trainers who use women riders use them if they are winning. Nobody is going to use any jockey who is not winning at least some of the time. What people don't realize is that in order to win a jockey has to have a good horse under her and has to give that horse a good ride. The horse is an athlete equal to its rider.

My early advisers used to tell me, "You'll get attention in this industry by bringing in the long shots, so go out there and find a way to ride them to victory." This created a lot of "positive thinking," which translated into "positive riding" on all my horses, and even though the percentages are not high, long shots (at least in terms of the betting) do come in and get noticed. Races are set up in so many different ways; I just have to be mentally astute and ride the best route for me and my horse.

Role Models

When I first came to the racetrack I remember seeing Karen Rogers. I watched her ride and work out the horses. I was in total awe, a woman riding. Could that be me one day? At the time Angel Cordero was the leading rider and winning everything in sight. I idolized him and followed his career. Jorge Velesquez also was an influence, but Karen Rogers was—Wow!

Julie Krone and I coincidentally decided to tackle New York on a permanent basis at the same time, the winter of 1990–91. Julie really opened the door for female jockeys by winning and being on television and being in the national media spotlight.

A lot more women are in racing now than there used to be. I think it is an issue of support for most young girls wanting to enter the business. A lot of parents think it's not a good life for their daughters. It's a cultural "misthought." "It's not a life for girls; it's a rough life," they say. And that is not really true. I have met the most prestigious people in the world through horse racing. I probably wouldn't have met them had I been in another career. People don't realize though, that jockeys have to start at the bottom, as in any field and for us it's in the barns, on the backstretch, and at 6:00 A.M. working out the horses. Jockeys can't just walk in at the top.

I've witnessed enormous changes in the years that I have been riding. When I first came to

New York, the general feeling was that a female always had to do better than a male jockey to get a chance. If a trainer put me up on a horse to ride, I had better not make any mistakes because I wouldn't get a second chance. That produced a lot of pressure to be perfect, and no one can do that—be perfect every time—and all riders, even the accomplished ones, make mistakes. Nowadays, it's more equal. I just have to prove that I am as good as the guys if someone has an issue about that, not better, just as good, to get a chance.

Even the criticism from the fans has changed through the years. People who are betting their hard-earned money on horses used to blame every loss by a female jockey on her gender. They made this very clear by the names they used to call us after a race. Now, when female riders lose, the betting fans mostly criticize them not for "girl" faults, but for "jockey" faults, such as moving too soon in a race or getting boxed in behind horses, and that's progress in my eyes!

I hope I can be a good role model for women who want to get into this business. As a sideline, I did some modeling in my younger years, mostly endorsements. Riding has always been my

Modeling a line of gold jewelry at Saks Fifth Avenue. I really wasn't looking to model but thought it was important to have jockeys involved in endorsements just like other sports figures were. *Courtesy of Jamie Phillips.*

Diane Nelson

number one business, and modeling was an extension of that. I wasn't really planning to model but to have my name and face used as a jockey for product endorsements. I thought it was really important to have jockeys involved in things like that, just like football players and other sports figures were. I was signed on to the Ford Modeling Agency for awhile. It was a tough market. My agent wanted me to go on and on with it; I didn't. I would say to him, "I am a jockey; that's who I am."

I get a fair amount of fan mail. I used to get tons up in New England and, of course, when I got hurt, I was flooded. One housewife in the New York area writes to me constantly. Her kids write to me too, and they all watch me race on the replay program at 6:30 P.M. every night on television. I'm very touched by them.

Of course, everyone wants to know how I got started in this business. They also ask, "How does it feel to win?" I try to answer that, but it is really hard to verbalize the feeling. I say, "Wonderful, great," every adjective I can think of. But I always remind people that the most important thing for me is to be able to do what I love and to earn a living doing it.

I am asked questions such as, "How does it feel to be a woman in a man's sport?" And I say, "Who said it was a man's sport?" The girls that ride, including me, don't think, "Gee I'm a girl. Am I supposed to be riding?" They just do it because they love it. Another thing that people have expressed is the notion that females who ride in this business need to be rough and tough and to project that image in order to compete. In fact, I hear this a lot from aspiring women jockeys. They feel they need to be like that. It is not so.

People say to me, "Oh you have hair!" I tell them, "I didn't have to cut all my hair off to ride." I get asked, "Do you eat?" I've always been light, so I don't have to do anything crazy; I just eat healthy, fresh foods and lots of protein. When I'm busy, I burn it off, and when I'm slow, I cut back. It's self-maintenance. I'll eat a candy bar if I want to. I just have to know when to adjust myself.

The great feeling of winning on number seven. *Courtesy of Bob Coglianese.*

Great Women in the Sport of Kings

Career and Social Life Merge

After I straightened myself out mentally and emotionally after my divorce, I took on a lot of work and moved around a lot through the year, riding at Monmouth in the summer, the Meadowlands in the fall, and Aqueduct in the winter. I took an apartment with my best friend from childhood in New York. My mounts in the winter held me through the summer months financially, so I didn't have to do so much traveling. This stabilized me even more emotionally.

I met Butch Lenzini, a trainer whom I became involved with romantically at this time. He encouraged me and was a wonderful stabilizer to me, as I was to him. He was also wanting not to move around so much from track to track. He was a famous trainer long before I met him. At the time we met he was in transition with new horses and new owners as clients, so it was good for both

Rows and rows of jockey silks that represent by color and design the ownership of the horses I ride. *Courtesy of Scooter Davidson.*

of us that we got together. We had a lot of success together, including seven wins in a row on a horse named Boom Towner. We were involved until his death in 1996.

During the five years that I was with Butch, my parents had become involved in the horse business, too. They were very successful in the plant nursery business, and my brother took over their business. My mother and father got into breeding horses first as a hobby and then as a business. They had many successes with horses that Butch trained for them, and the whole experience brought us closer as a family. My father started coming to the races more, and I enjoyed sharing those times with him.

I've been riding some really nice horses in New York lately and have been up to Saratoga for the last two summers and have won up there a lot. As far as my career visions go, I have a funny story to tell you. When I was riding at Rockingham Park, I was doing dozens of interviews as the leading rider at twenty years of age. The journalists would always ask me, "So how long do you think you will be riding?" And as a twenty year old I would say, "Oh I'm sure I won't be riding when I'm thirty!" Well, I thought when I turned thirty I wouldn't be able to do this. I'm thirty-one now and truthfully things couldn't be better. I don't even think about quitting or retiring to do something else.

A lot of the girl jockeys stop riding to have a family. They say, "That's it. I'm stopping riding to have a family now," but I see a lot of them are coming back to riding after they have had their children. I recently rode in an all-girl jockey challenge at Remmington Park. We were all in the jockey's room, and everyone seemed to be talking about their kids. I thought to myself, soon we are going to have to have jockey day care; this is racing in the nineties.

In my spare time, or my slow time at the track, I take horses that aren't doing so well in their racing at the track and quiet them. I retrain them as show horses and find them new homes in the process. This makes me happy, and I find when I'm happy, in my off time, I show up to work with a smile on my face, which perpetuates a winning attitude with my coworkers, trainers, owners, and the horses. I even took lessons to jump horses. Can you imagine a jockey taking post lessons? I did; it was great. I find it very fulfilling to rehabilitate some of the horses who just couldn't take to the track. It takes a lot of time with each horse to do this, but it is just another way of showing my love of horses.

Luckily, there is a market out there for retired racehorses, both formally and within the inner circles of the industry among the trainers and owners. The Thoroughbred Retirement Association even teaches inmates from some of the prisons located near the retirement farms how to care for the horses with amazing results for both the horses and the inmates. The closeness, the bonding, and the caring that happen between the inmates and the horses are incredible!

People always ask me about my social life. I usually answer, "What social life?" One thing, if I am going to be in this business, I have to really love it. It takes over my life. I have set days that I work. I don't go on vacations unless I get a suspension for riding a foul. I can't go away on weekends, plan to be at weddings or birthday parties, and we work on all the holidays. My schedule makes my friends outside of the track nuts! Even though I've been riding for a long time, people still say to me, "So when are you going to stop and do other things?" But I'm not stopping and have no remorse about my chosen life. I had a ton of friends back in school of which I remain friendly with one. Most of my friends now are people I've met from age seventeen on, horse people friends. My dear friend from childhood, however, gets a big reaction when she tells others of her friendship with me. They say, "You know a jockey? I can't believe you know a real jockey!"

Socially, most of my friends are in the horse industry. I developed a whole lifestyle with new family and friends who have the same interests and days off I do. We are never off when other people are, like on weekends and holidays, so it's really hard to maintain a social life with people who are on a different schedule. Yes, I still get invited to all the social events I used to before I started riding professionally, only now the sentiment from my friends and family is, "Diane, we understand. If you can make it, great." One of the social settings I enjoy is when Frank Lovato, a fellow jockey, sings at the local clubs. He put together a musical band of people from the track, and they play the clubs wherever the racing is going on, even up at Saratoga. I go because I know I'll be going someplace where there are people I enjoy being around and people who have the same interests as I do. There is a lot of dating within the industry. What guy is going to date me if I can't go out on weekends? But it's a great community, and when things go well and when times go bad, they are there for you.

11

Diane Nelson

Julie Krone. *Courtesy of Roberta Fineberg, author and photographer of* City Riders.

Julie Krone

As a teenager in 1978 in Eau Claire, Michigan, Julie watched on television as jockey Steve Cauthen won the Belmont Stakes, the third race of the Triple Crown. This was the deciding factor that turned Julie from accomplished rider (riding horses since the age of two) into the most famous woman jockey of modern times with a list of "firsts" that towers over her 4'10" frame and includes the winning of the 125th running of the Belmont Stakes aboard 14:1 long shot Colonial Affair in 1993. She was also the first woman to ride in the Breeder's Cup back in 1988 and the first woman to reach two thousand career wins in 1990.

Even though her picture and career heights have graced the pages of *Newsweek, Sports Illustrated,* and hundreds of newspapers worldwide and she has appeared on the *Tonight Show* and has been honored by President George Bush on National Women's Sports Day, Julie is still out there at 6:00 A.M., six days a week, prepping horses for the trainers she rides for in the afternoon races. She is a fine example of the saying that "success is a journey, not a destination."

Where It All Started

I, Julieann Louise Krone, was born in Benton Harbor, Michigan, on July 24, 1963. My riding career began on my father's back, but I soon moved from my dad, Donald Krone, to my dog Twiggy, and then to Dixie, my Shetland pony.

I don't remember a time when I didn't ride. My mother, Judi, lifted me onto a horse when I was just two when a woman came to look at a horse she was thinking of buying from our farm in Eau Claire, Michigan. The horse trotted off with me on him and after Mom realized nervously what had happened, she saw me reach down, grab the horse's reins, and turn the horse back to her.

Mom taught me to be patient and understanding of all animals, of which there were many on the farm. As she was teaching me to ride, Mom would say, "You can't make him (the horse) do what he doesn't want to do. Think about what's in his mind, then encourage him to do his best." It was a lesson I would never forget.

Early Independence

By the time I was four years old Mom had rigged up a pulley in one of the trees so that I could lift my saddle off the ground and onto the horse's back. By the time I was six years old I was allowed to ride several miles away from home on my own.

I didn't like school and homework because they took me away from the horses. Although I wasn't very successful in school, I was a star in the show ring. In the summertime Mom and I traveled throughout Michigan to compete in horse shows. By September of each year my wall was full of ribbons for trail riding, show jumping, and dressage.

When I was fifteen years old, my parents divorced, and I became even closer to my mom. In 1979 I persuaded my mother to spend the spring break at Churchill Downs, home of the Kentucky Derby. I had already decided years before that I wanted to be a jockey, and I wanted to show her what life at a racetrack was like.

Once in Louisville, Mom found a job and forced me to go off on my own, saying, "Nobody will hire a kid who looks ten years old if her momma is with her." Wandering through the stables, I met Clarence and Donna Picou. Clarence had been a jockey in his younger years and now trained horses. He asked me what I could do, and I said, "I can do anything with a horse—ride, brush, groom—you name it." I was hired.

Trading in Teenage Years

Although many girls my age were wearing makeup and going on dates, I had my mind on one thing, riding, and one hero, eighteen-year-old Steve Cauthen who won the Kentucky Derby in 1978 and whom I had watched on television. I tried to imitate his riding style—head down, seat up, back level. So even in the dead of winter I galloped my Arabian horse and wrote about my progress in my diary. I know I can be the greatest jockey in the world, I wrote.

My mother let me move to my grandmother's house in Tampa, Florida, in 1980 so I would be able to look for work at the Tampa Bay Downs Racetrack and keep my promise to her that I would get my high school diploma.

I met Jerry Pace at the racetrack even before I was fully unpacked. "So you want to be a jockey," Jerry Pace said, smiling. "No," I answered, "I'm going to be a jockey." So he put me on a horse to exercise it. By the fifth day at Tampa I was able to get my jockey's license. In my first race on a horse called Tiny Star I just missed first place; however, I brought Lord Farkle across the finish line first shortly thereafter.

Horses, Helpers, and Heroines

After being at Tampa Racetrack for a while, I met a young women, Julie Snellings, who worked in the track official's office. One day when my new friend gave me more advice than I felt I needed, I snapped at her and said, "If you know so much, why don't you ride?" Then she rolled out from behind the desk . . . in a wheelchair. My mouth dropped open. Julie Snellings had been one of the best female riders on the Maryland-Delaware circuit until a horse fell on her and she was paralyzed in 1977.

Julie and I became friends, and it wasn't long before she introduced me to her former agent in Maryland, Chick Lang, Jr., who started to get me "long shot" mounts on horses at the Maryland Racetrack. The male riders did not take kindly to me at their track and did many things to discourage me, trying to get me to return to Michigan. But a trainer, Bud Delp, let me ride, and

I won three races in a row for him. Julie Snellings moved to the Delaware Racetrack to work, moved in with me, and gave me encouragement and her old riding silks to wear, which brought me a lot of luck and work!

On February 26, 1982, I set a track record as the first female rider in Maryland to win four races in one day. My apprentice years were over. I knew that no woman had ever become famous in horse racing, yet that was what I planned to do.

I moved up to the New Jersey circuit and on to a determined young agent, Larry Cooper. "Work, get me more work," I would tease Larry as he drove me from one track to another while I napped in the car. I became the first female rider to win the racing season at the Atlantic City Racetrack. Then it was on to the Meadowlands and big-time trainers such as John Forbes and Peter Shannon hired me .

Fans and Plans

Even though I was winning races often, I would pass by racing fans at the track and sometimes hear things like "Go home and wash the dishes" or "You don't ride like no girl!"

But that didn't discourage me. At nineteen years of age I had my own apartment, had new friends, and had won 155 races, making more than one million dollars in prize money for the horse owners. As a jockey I kept only 10 percent of the winnings; then I had to pay my agent 25 percent of that. Still, I felt rich and famous as newspaper articles and appearances on the *Tonight Show* came my way. President George Bush honored me on National Women's Sports Day.

I went on to ride at New York's Belmont Park and won. I had a few mishaps along the way, riding accidents and worries about my mother's illness, but my desire to be the best never left me.

Honors

When 1986 ended, I had won more than two million dollars in prize money. I was the leading rider in 1987 at Monmouth Park and the Meadowlands racetracks. As my victories began to add up, I thought I might pass the record held by my friend, P. J. Cooksey. P. J. had 1,204 victories and was the leading female jockey in the country. By February 29, 1988, I had won 1,199 races. On March 6 I had only one race to go to beat P. J.'s record. I rode a horse named Squawter to the front of the pack and stayed there to break the record! Articles were written about me in *Newsweek, People,* and *Sports Illustrated* magazines.

All the honors I've received have made me happy. Everyone has told me how well I've done, yet I can't help but think they still mean "as a woman."

I don't want to be just the best female jockey in the world; I want to be the best jockey. But my "firsts" as a woman kept piling up. I was the first female to win the riding titles, (the rider with the most wins during a meet) at both Monmouth Park and the Meadowlands in 1987, 1988, and 1989. On December 13, 1987, I was the first female to win four races in one day in New York. In 1992 I was the first woman to top the standings at Belmont Park with 73 wins out of 370 mounts, a 20 percent

Julie Krone

In the winner's circle after winning the 125th running of the Belmont Stakes aboard a long shot, Colonial Affair. I am the first woman in history not only to ride in the Belmont Stakes but to win this Triple Crown race. *Courtesy of Barbara D. Livingston.*

win average. In 1988 I was the first woman to ride in the Breeders Cup. On October 26, 1990, I became the first woman to reach 2,000 career wins. In 1991 I was the first woman to ride in the Belmont Stakes. And on June 5, 1993, I, Julie Krone, made history capturing the win aboard Colonial Affair, a 14:1 shot in the 125th running of the Belmont Stakes, part of racing's Triple Crown. The horse brought to his owners $444,540 for the 2 min. 29 sec. race, and I took home my 10 percent and four autographed programs that the other riders in the race signed for me as souvenirs.

In Retrospect and
Looking Toward the Future

I think sometimes athletes are looked at by the general public one-sidedly. It bothers me that they look at or associate with only the athletic "versions" of competitors; they don't understand or realize there is a real person in there with a real life, a life that includes traumatizing experiences that have adverse effects on her positive attitudes and all the times she has to grab her bootstraps, so to speak. It's not always a smooth ride.

I've come to know my maturity level. When I first started out as an athlete, I had a desire and was driven by a feeling. Success was also very simple because I was able to just hang onto the feathers of the "bird" of success and it took me all over. I think that of most successful people who are really young, very few will ever have intact the faculties of being a "good" person with emotions such as empathy and respect. They have a higher than "life-thing" going, and that's fine for someone who is doing something that takes a lot of courage.

When I see younger people and they do have some kind of maturity to them, I admire that because I never had it. I was always very narcissistic, never hurtful or mean to anyone, just very self-centered about everything I did. When I left home and was out on my own and trying to prove I was good with horses, people would say they would do a certain thing on a horse, and I would say, "Oh, I could do that." They would say, "Well, you go ahead and do it, then." I always could do it, so I developed "confidence."

When I was younger, it was obvious that I had an "altercation" with drugs, which complements what I just said about not having a maturity level and proper values. I was nineteen or twenty then, and in looking back, it was not anything that my parents did or didn't do; I just lacked a lot of maturity as far as my "person" went. In fact, my parents did a really good job. I love them both dearly, and I credit 50 percent of my success to my mother. When I said, "Mom, I want to be a jockey," she told the veterinarian, and he told her to go hit me on the head. She took me to the racetrack!

My mom and I.
Courtesy of Barbara D. Livingston.

Julie Krone

I'm a lot prouder of the person I am now. People all along in my life at the racetrack helped me grow up and taught me values as a person. When I see them now, instead of giving them a casual hello, I just want to give them a big hug and thank them for putting time into me because I was such a jerk then. When I talk to some of them, they insist I wasn't as bad as I thought I was, which is always a relief. When I run into people I knew when I was younger, I say, "Tell me I wasn't like that."

I think when a person becomes a certain age, she suddenly goes on a quest, a search for herself. I realize racing has given me grounding, a gravity; it's helped me so much to be a "person." I make the analogy about someone who has been flighty and inconsistent in her life who settles down and has kids. The kids and the care they need keep her focused and in one place in her head. Racing has done that for me: I always have to show up; I can never be less than 100 percent; I have to work early mornings and all day. I guess I could say I have to become obsessive about my work. That's what I did, and it turned me around. Racing provides a chance to be physical too, which is a big outlet.

It's also fun. I get to be an athlete every day although there are days when the temperature is 30 deg. and the wind is blowing 20 mph and I say to myself, "What am I doing?" and "Boy, I wish I wore heels and sat behind a desk somewhere." But a lot of other days are full of accomplishments, and I don't even have to win a race. For example, I might ride for a trainer or owner who raised the horse himself and the horse comes in, even in fourth place, and gets a check (makes money). Or I can ride four horses for the same person in one day and get checks for all four of them and some of them are long shots. Days don't always have to hold winners. If I were a gambler and was looking at it from a gambling aspect, "win, place, and show" would be all that mattered. But as I am in it every day, I am working with people whose livelihoods depend on breaking even, at least, with their horses, and the fact that I am participating in that effort is a really good feeling.

Before I "grew up" emotionally, I would come in third or fourth in a race and wouldn't walk away with the same satisfaction that I do now with an appreciation of and empathy for people's situations. When I was "younger," I would walk away and say, "Ah, I didn't win," or "I could have ridden the horse that won." I didn't have the knowledge that I could go off with a nice feeling instead, a feeling that I did well for somebody's horse today and could walk to the parking lot a happy person. The love of horses has always held me together. Diane Nelson and I have spent a lot of time together, just riding horses and being on our jumpers. I think a lot of jockeys have never been on any horse except a racehorse. Diane and I can jump on horses bareback and ride them into a lake somewhere. When we go with our horses into the show ring, we may not win blue ribbons, but we laugh a lot and we keep both our stirrups and don't lose our reins. We try to make every moment count.

If a ten-year-old girl came to me and said, "I want to be a jockey," I would say, "Oh, that's good." I wouldn't pay too much attention to it because I feel it's an age when there is not a lot of dedication to particular things, and if there is, it's most likely to change in the teenage years. I run

My jumper horse, Peter Rabbit, and I enjoying a relaxing afternoon. *Courtesy of Barbara D. Livingston.*

into kids now who come up to me and say, "Remember when I came to you and told you I wanted to be a jockey?" And I see them downtown hanging out with boys all the time, dressing "grunge," and not doing a thing about their riding. So everybody goes through stages of what she wants to do when she grows up.

Once in a while certain little girls lead a different life even at a young age. When these girls get home from school, they throw their backpacks down, pay no attention to their schoolwork or homework, and run to their horses or to their riding lessons. It's almost an obsession, their horses. They can't get away from it, and everything else in life is an inconvenience.

To be around those little girls is to pick up on their "differentness" quickly. Anything that takes time away from their horses becomes a burden—their clothes, homework, boys, parties, and so forth. They have only a small amount of physical strength at that age but they have a real caring for all animals. In fact, there is a little imbalance there at times because they seem to care more for animals than for people. The animals have more value to them than people do. It's an early natural human survival tendency that they have oriented toward animals rather than people. I pick up on that trait in them because I was that way as a kid and it is very characteristic of girls who go on to ride professionally. Adults are educated to accept the value of things and people, but children may go naturally toward things. I see horses that have peculiar habits; adults will say, "Oh, this horse just annoys me so." That special little girl will take to that horse, accept it and all the "bad" things that people were saying he did. Two to three weeks later after being with the little girl, he's not doing them anymore. It's not a scientific thing; it's a love thing.

I have written down a saying for success that I follow: "Pick one thing and stick with it." In my personal life it is my husband; professionally and socially it is horses. I don't have a lot of social time, maybe one-quarter of a "normal" person's, and if I put that into horses, well. . . . Actually, I love being with my show horses. It's something I want to become really good at because it's

Julie Krone

Loving my show horse.
Courtesy of Barbara D. Livingston.

something I would like to become involved with when I retire from racing. I would like to run a pony club or a school for girls with their jumpers, really helping girls.

I learned some facts from the Women's Sports Foundation that make me mad. In curriculums girls are allowed to go to fifth and sixth grade competing with boys, developing feelings of team and group spirit. They ride in all the same clubs. Then when the girls hit a certain age, they are expelled from the groups. It's very painful. I know what that pain feels like, and I think it's very unfair. The boys are offered sports up to higher grades than girls are. When a school, which for a kid is one of the most influential representations of adult organizations in her life does something like that, she doesn't know what to think. She is going to have a split in her emotions because of it and can develop attitudes that she will carry through life. Somebody needs to save somebody along the way. It's the 1990s, and if I can affect one hundred lives by the time I'm fifty years old, that will be doing a pretty good job. They'll affect one hundred more, and so on. Things will change.

Looking back, things that happened to me were unfair to girls in general. The way I handled it was to make-believe it wasn't happening. I didn't participate in it emotionally or physically, and obviously, it worked for me somehow. When a situation presented itself, I would say, "I am not going to feed into that. I'm going to do what I want to do." It worked for me, but I also understand that that approach isn't for everybody and that sometimes people aren't strong enough or capable enough to exhibit that kind of behavior in a given situation.

Fortunately, I had a natural instinct to do things that way. I poured every single inch of my life into horses. In a promotion once a fictional person was cut open and the doctors found—let's say, he was an aspiring basketball player—a basketball inside him instead of a heart. Well, I'd probably have a heart, but it would beat like a horse's feet, "gallop, gallop, gallop."

Horses have always been my focus and have helped me "get focused." I had a little pony that was such a challenge and took a lot, if not all, of my time when I was younger. But when she was right, we won every blue ribbon there was to win. I had to be so in tune with everything she was thinking. My mom is definitely part horse! In fact, that's her sign in Chinese astrology. She would say all the right things to encourage me, "Well, we can get you another pony if you want," which only made me try harder with the pony I had. It became a real challenge to me. "I can do it, I can do it with this pony," I stubbornly said.

My mother never had to really encourage me to stick with something; I just did it automatically. When I broke my ankle, the doctors said they would have to fuse it. When I inquired, "How do you fuse an ankle?" they said, "Well, you fuse it at an angle with your toe pointed down a little." And I said, "Well, no, you can't do that because then I can't ride. I would rather walk around on my heel when I have to because I spend more time on a horse's back than I do on the ground!"

Horseback riding of any kind requires a lot of courage. You also have to be capable of a silent communication. Not everyone can be great with a horse. A lot of people are good with a horse, but not great. A deep, silent communication goes on. I think it was Shakespeare who wrote that "no secret is so close as that between a horse and its rider." There is more truth to that concept than most people realize.

Let's say I get on a horse and can communicate with it and can get it to do something. Then someone else gets on and says, "How did you do that?" Now I have to communicate verbally how I did that. So not only do I have to be talented as a silent communicator and be able to read the look in the horse's eye and the flick of its ears and its body language but I have to translate it into words that people can understand. There is a guy named Buck Brenanman, a cowboy of sorts, who can take a horse that can't be caught even in a pen and in fifteen minutes he can have that horse walking around with his nose in his armpit without a lead rope on it. These are the levels of communication a horse is capable of. Buck can also tell someone in words how to do it.

Girls can realize those kinds of levels of communication with a horse at a very early age. It is a never-ending process, almost a colored spectrum of learning. Adults can turn kids onto horses and they'll ride for awhile, but very few have that obsession.

The first time I got paid for racing a horse, I thought, "Wow! You're paying me to do this!" Eighteen years later, I accept it. It's the opposite of when I used to show horses; that cost me money to do. So now, when I have a good week riding at the track, I say, "Okay, now I can afford to go back to a horse show this weekend." In my mind it's a treat to do a pleasurable thing. I set myself up. If I win five races this week, I'll go because it's going to cost me. The majority of girls who show horses don't make the connection in their heads with becoming involved in racing. They might know other girls who gallop at the racetrack or for trainers. They might, if they are in the city, go by the off-track

Julie Krone

betting (OTB) and say, "Oh look at those girls, they're jockeys," or they might pick up this book and say, "Oh, girls are jockeys all the time. I can do that!"

The first time I went to the racetrack I had to climb a fence to get in. So it hasn't been all that easy, but it's not been all that hard either. I showed horses. People are always trying to compare the treatment of show horses to that of racehorses, and I don't think it's fair. Every foot and step of a horse in a show situation is governed. The horse is picked apart and analyzed. Every movement it makes is measured by a human being. The horse must feel inside like it's just got to get away somehow. If I turn a horse loose after he's shown all day, he will just run and bust out as if to shake the day off of himself. So there is a stress level in horses; their emotions get taxed.

Racehorses are allowed to experience all the very natural things a horse would in the wild—the flight and fight, their natural wildness. They are free to jump around and kick. One never takes that away from them because mentally that's what makes them bold and brave on the racetrack. So who's to say whether show horses or racehorses are treated better? Racehorses are pampered at the track: "She likes this. Don't touch her butt; she doesn't like that. She sleeps on three feet of hay in her stall," and so on.

I think in the 1960s women did things to prove they could do things. What do I think it takes in the 1990s for a woman to be successful riding either show horses or racehorses? Well, to make it simple, they have to have good mind-body control and have to be good at reading silent signals. They have to be fit mentally and physically and be able to perform physically as athletes. I'm not a bragger; I think I'm very humble about my success, especially because I've been injured so many times. I've gone through the natural process of life and things like that. I was very fortunate since I was little to be a "gifted" athlete. I could go to the circus, watch people stand up on a horse that was cantering around the ring, and go home and do it. I could do anything with my body, and I could control my body with my mind.

All the female jockeys I know are very good athletes in another area of sports as well. Diane Nelson is an incredible swimmer, and she plays baseball really well also. Any female or male jockey does or did something on the side that is really outstanding athletically, even at an earlier age. A lot of the great jockeys were good wrestlers in school, which takes a lot of agility and mind control. The same applies to show jumper athletes. All the girls on the U.S. Equestrian team say the same thing; control of mind over body is important. A rider has to be aware of so many little things as well as major ones when riding a horse.

I'm always very flattered when people, especially young girls, come up to me and ask me things. A lot of my answers to them are replays of what I've told people before, but once in a while one girl is a little different and there is a chemistry between us. Most of the time she is young, but some have been older. I respond because all of a sudden something carries over, maybe an expression or a word she uses, something is a little different. Some girls I have brought to my house and taught them to ride better. One little girl wrote to me when my ankle was broken, and there was something different about her letter. I got thousands of letters when I was hurt; my basement looked like it was full of Santa Claus's bags. Her name was Shannon Driscoll. She was nine years old then; she's thirteen now. When I read her letter, I said, "I'm going to write to her right now and invite her to my house." I noticed she had put her phone number on the letter, so I called her and spoke to her mother first. Shannon came over. She was so horse crazy then and still is; I ran into her at the mall a while back.

Early in my career, I didn't make a big point of the fact that I was a girl jockey. I was just a jockey; I wanted to be known as just a jockey. I dropped the girl part. I was genderless; I was just an athlete. Now I'm very comfortable with being a woman jockey. Back then, I probably had that attitude to protect myself. For the next generation it won't even be an issue. All of us female jockeys present ourselves in feminine ways; it's all very natural.

I'm married now, and I love children. My husband is such an internally strong person. He was raised by his mother and had a sister ten years older than he was. I think he was raised with a great "female version of life" from his mom and sister. He is able to sit me down and say, "You know, you're being a real jerk. You need to straighten up." But he can also sit down and say, "You know, I was a real jerk, and I'm sorry," and we can both sit back and laugh like kids. Our relationship is perfect.

Matt, my husband, and I actually knew each other for years at the racetrack before we even considered going out. In fact, I hated him and he hated me. I thought he was a stuck-up, steroid playboy. He lived up at Saratoga as a kid. He groomed and walked horses and then got a basketball scholarship to college. He's 6'4"; I'm 4'10". He still worked at the racetrack up there during the summers of his college years as a Pinkerton guard. The Pinkertons walk riders through the crowd onto the track itself, and that's what he did. He used to take Angel Cordero and Mike Smith, and then they asked me if I wanted him to walk me through the crowd. I said, "No." He thought I was a snob. We socialized separately with different people up there, but anybody who knew us both kept saying, "You guys have got to get together." So he started to call me. I got to know him a lot better; we went out on a date. On our first date everything we would say to each other, we'd answer, "Me, too!" We were exactly alike. The day of our wedding, we said, "I do," and I won on my mount two races later. We have a great life together. I have a problem with numbers—I think it's called "discalculus"—so I just save my money. I love that my husband takes care of our finances. This is the opposite of my friend, jockey Donna Barton; she is totally independent with a capital *I*.

I guess I've retained some of my childlike qualities. I think a lot of the female jockeys feel a bit of "adult abandonment" because it's almost necessary. Even in the most mature, self-representing-type jockeys there is a slight edge of childlike behavior. It's impossible not to show it. If Angel Cordero, who is in his fifties came in here right now I would swear he was fifteen years old because of his energy and bouncing around the room. Mike Smith and I played tag in the post parade one day. I was on a horse without a pony companion, and he was on a horse with a pony companion. I galloped by him and hit him and yelled, "You're it!" He couldn't tag me back, so I went by him

Julie Krone

again. He said, "I'm gonna get my rubberbands out when I get back to the room." I said, "No, you're not!" He said, "I swear you're like an eleven year old."

You know, I hit my head really hard on the side of a tree when I was twelve, and I was like this when I was twelve. Generally speaking, I'm like this all the time. Maybe I've stayed twelve and don't realize it. Actually I'm fine with being thirty-three. I'm happily riding and happily married. I would like to have children someday and have a farm for them to enjoy as I did, but for now I have a racing family of top jockeys and trainers and love being a spokesperson for Thoroughbred racing as well as an accomplished athlete who happens to be a woman.

Paula Keim-Bruno. *Courtesy of Equi-Photo, Inc.*

Paula Keim-Bruno

When Paula hears the expression, "Life begins at forty," she can honestly say for her it began at thirty with her jockey career on Thoroughbreds. The daughter of an orthopedic doctor and a nurse, Paula, also a registered nurse, was not afraid to get out there and start a new career.

Instead of working her way up at smaller, easier racetracks, Paula jumped right onto the New York racing circuit in 1995 and finished fourth on her very first mount, a horse named Overtake, for famed trainer Leo O'Brien. Getting a lot of attention for booting home long shots early in her career, in less than three years, Paula has won more than one dozen stakes races at Saratoga, Belmont, and other prestigious racetracks. She has also won the respect of other jockeys, both male and female, trainers such as Alan Jerkens, and sports figures, most notably, baseball coach Don Zimmer.

Born with the Love of Horses

I started life in Winnipeg, Canada. My father is an orthopedic surgeon and at the time was doing a hand fellowship up there. I'm the third born in the family. My mom was a nurse. My sister, Sharon, is four years older, my brother, Steve, three years older. They were born in the States. We moved around quite a lot. My father was in the army, and we lived in California, Illinois, and Kansas where my younger brother, Greg, was born four years after I was. Most of my childhood memories, however, are of growing up in Tenefly, New Jersey.

At age three—ride, ride, ride!
Courtesy of the Keim-Bruno family.

I loved horses. I was born with the love of horses. My mother loved horses. Even at two and three years of age, I have pictures of me on horses, and my parents have told me I was most excited when I saw horse vans on the highway as a toddler. I would yell, "Horses! Horses!"

I started riding lessons at age seven over at Knockeen Farm in Rockleigh, New Jersey. The man who owned it, Dick Widger, used to ride steeplechase horses in Ireland. He had a very heavy Irish accent and was one of eleven kids. He had come to the States with the steeplechase horses and with Leo O'Brien and Joe Murphy. Mr. Widger played a big role in my life then and still does now. I was begging my parents at that time for my own pony, and my father told me that if I got good grades, I could get a pony. I wasn't that great a student. I was very hyperactive. I was very much a tomboy, hated wearing dresses, and was always getting into fights with boys. All I wanted to do was ride.

I got my first pony when I was nine. Her name was Petunia, and she was the greatest pony I have ever known. When I first got her, I used to fall off her all the time. We had an outside course that we used for jumping. After the first jump it was a little downhill, and she would put her head down, not to buck me off but to eat a little grass along the way. My older sister and mother rode,

My first pony, Petunia,
and I at nine years old.
Courtesy of the Keim-Bruno family.

Great Women in the Sport of Kings

too. My sister got on Petunia to straighten her out and to help me with her. Mr. Widger would jump up and down, and yell and scream about what we were doing wrong. If he wasn't yelling at me, I didn't feel he cared. He had two daughters, Mary and Ann, and a son, Dick, Jr. I was very close to his daughters, and his wife, Judy, was like my other mother. I still call her my "stable mom."

So my childhood was really wrapped up in horses. My sister was a very good rider. She was a competitive jumper. By the time I was eleven years old I wanted to be a jockey.

Answered Prayers

I used to pray, "God, please don't let me grow too tall." I didn't. My father was only 5'7½", my mom 5'4". I got lucky; the genes were there. My sister is 5'2". She could have been a jockey, but she didn't want to be one. So I'm 4'11" now. Back in third grade I was 3'11". I took gymnastics in school and, of course, continued my riding. I also continued jumping horses through my teens because that was what I was exposed to. When I was fifteen, I qualified for the Madison Square Garden National Horse Show, and the ASPCA and National Horse shows in Harrisburg, Pennsylvania, and Washington, D.C. I was the youngest participant up until that time to qualify for the Madison Square Garden show. This was the biggest thing in my life. I was a junior rider and rode a horse named Without a Doubt, but we called him Mikey. My parents were very supportive of my riding; in fact, we rode as a family. I started fox hunting with my mother at age nine. Mr. Widger would get a lot of horses in for sale, so he let me get up on a lot of them. This gave me experience with different horses and situations. But I still wanted to be a jockey. I went out and bought a jockey cap with the silk covers and wore it for two years straight. I wouldn't take it off. My mom had to take it to the one-hour dry cleaners and bring it back!

When I graduated from high school, my parents insisted that I have something to fall back on. So I went to nursing school and got my degree. I worked as a nurse for two and one half years in New York, which was actually very good for me, and I didn't have to give up my riding. I worked the evening shifts as a nurse so I could ride during the day. I felt (at twenty-two) that I was missing out on a career with what I loved, horses.

Around that same time, my father bought a farm in Pawling, New York. I enrolled at Delhi University and studied equine animal husbandry and breeding. Next to my father's farm was a Thoroughbred training center. My father built a small barn on his land, and my mother had a few horses there. I graduated from Delhi and went to work for John Hettinger at his Thoroughbred training center. Eventually, I was able to buy myself a couple of ponies at a sale down in Virginia. A friend of mine helped me pick them out. I lived at my father's farm and started to breed ponies.

My first crop turned out really well. I broke the babies and then sold them. One of the foals turned out to be the third leading pony hunter in the nation. I was so proud.

I continued to work for John at the training center for one year and a half, breaking the two year olds and galloping horses in the morning. This was my first exposure to actual racehorses. For me it was a difficult time because I had been on hunters and jumpers, and now had to shift from

Paula Keim-Bruno

major control to letting the horses go. I also kept my little breeding business going, buying and selling ponies. I kept the nursing career alive as well. I worked at a nursing home right around the corner from the training center. It allowed me to keep my breeding business going. The nursing home let me work three nights a week from 5:00 P.M. to midnight.

As my breeding business got bigger, I found myself in trouble with the zoning board. We were zoned residential, so they shut me down. I had to sell all my ponies and I went down to work for Jay Shuttleworth riding hunters and jumpers. I worked for him for a couple of years. I was back buying and selling horses and even went to Europe with him to do some purchasing. After that I went back to work for Mr. Widger. After a short time he decided to sell his farm. When he did I went to work managing another farm. It was there I met Barbara Milanese whose husband had bought a property in Wyckoff, New Jersey.

Barbara asked me if I knew anyone who would be interested in leasing a property, a small barn with twelve stalls, a little indoor and outdoor ring, and a small paddock. I said, "In Wyckoff?" She said, "Why don't you come and look?" I told her I didn't really have the money to start up another business at the time but I went up to look anyway. The place was beautiful. I told her if I heard of anyone interested, I would let her know.

A couple of months passed and then Barbara called, told me she had bought a horse, and asked if I would be willing to help her start up a business there by being a worker. So I went over there and it was a beautiful situation. Before long I was back doing what I loved to do full time, working with the horses.

It was no time at all until we were boarding, buying, and selling horses. I was doing all the hard work myself which didn't bother me at all since I had done that ever since I was a girl. We were also making a living. Winter was coming and we had fifteen horses. I realized we needed some outside help, so I hired Steve Oliwa.

And Life Unfolds Exactly as It Should

Steve was a harness horse driver who wasn't racing Standardbreds at that time. He was ready to start work the day he drove up to the farm, so he moved onto the farm and started right in. He watched me ride every day and eventually said to me, "Why aren't you a jockey?" I said, "Steve, I'm thirty years old, too old." He said, "No you're not. There are people riding in their forties and fifties. You know, I have a friend named Jerry, and he has a couple of racehorses. I'll introduce you to him. I know he can help you."

My wheels were spinning! One day I went to see Jerry's horses run at Penn National Racetrack. He came out shortly after that to the farm and wound up buying a jumper from us. He watched me ride on the farm and said," All you need is an agent, you could do this. You could be a Thoroughbred jockey. You can definitely ride."

I called Mr. Widger for advice. I said, "Mr. Widger, I really, really want to be a jockey. I met this guy Jerry, and he thinks I can."

Mr. Widger replied, "Well Paula, you've always had this dream. I know you have, so I'm going to call Joe Murphy."

Joe Murphy, Mr. Widger, Jerry, and I met at Belmont Racetrack on February 19, 1995. I jumped right into the New York circuit. This was a most unusual place for an inexperienced jockey to begin. We went around to speak to some trainers and owners. We went to see Leo O'Brien and he started to put me on some horses. I met with a jockey agent named Eddy Fiffye who had Jean Cruget at the time. He took my book and started to be my agent as well.

One month later, on March 19, I rode and finished 4th on a horse for Leo O'Brien named OverTake. I rode a couple of more mounts and another month later I won my first race on one of Jerry's horses named Pago's Whim. He was a horse Jerry had just bought and he won first time out with me on him.

By now, Jerry and I had been dating a year and we decided to get married in October of 1995. When the summer after our marriage rolled around, Eddy Fiffye had to go down to Florida because his mother was sick. So with Mike Farro as my agent I rode at Monmounth Park, Atlantic City, and at the Meadowlands. This was a wonderful period for me although I found I had to make a big adjustment physically. I thought I was really fit from all the years of developing muscles in my arms, legs, and back. I thought I was fit enough to be a jockey full time. I wasn't.

Leo O'Brien helped me get fit, jockey fit. I would go out to Belmont at 4 A.M. and get on horses. I had strong muscles from all the years of riding, but this was completely different. The length of the stirrup was different on the saddle. On jumpers, a lot of the steering is done with your legs and to settle a horse your hands and legs work together. With racehorses, you ride in jacked-up irons and straddle their backs. I also did a lot of push-ups and worked with weights to develop these muscles.

I Lived My Dream

In the fall of 1995 I began really to roll at the Meadowlands meet, winning fourteen races. I went back in March of 1996, to Aqueduct Racetrack to ride Risk the House. She was a really nice filly, and I had won on her at the Meadowlands. I came to New York with the horse and she won; we won. I had a win on another horse that was brought over to Aqueduct shortly after that. I joined up with Marty Basile, an agent who had handled a number of apprentice jockeys in the past, and before I knew it, my racing career was soaring. H. Allen Jerkens, a Hall of Fame trainer, saw me in the mornings working other horses. I went up to him and said," Mr. Jerkens can I ask you a question?" "What?" he said. "Well, if you would let me get on some of your horses in the morning, I could get to know them a little bit. I could help you, and you could maybe help me." "I don't need any more help," he abruptly said. So I sadly said, "Oh, all right." He paused a minute and then said, "Come in the morning."

The next morning I was there at 6:00 A.M. I got on five horses for him. He didn't yell at me after any of them, so I knew I did okay. From then on I just showed up there every morning, and before long he started to name me on horses to ride in the afternoon at the races.

Paula Keim-Bruno

Behind the scenes before jockeys are called onto the racetrack to ride. After they put on protective clothing, silks, and helmets and affix the numbers of their horses on their sleeves, they have a moment to relax or talk. *Courtesy of Scooter Davidson.*

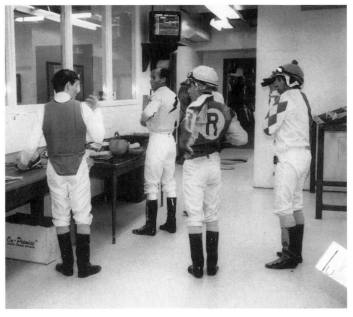

I won for him on Gentleness, a filly. She won by eight lengths. It was one of the only win photos I have where I'm not smiling because I was still in shock from going so fast! My relationship with Mr. Jerkens started to develop after that.

I found Mr. Jerkens very similar in demeanor to Mr. Widger, and I was very comfortable with that. Mr. Jerkens would even talk to me about my rides on horses other than the ones he trained. This was so helpful to me. When he would yell at me now and then about what I did on a horse, I wasn't shattered. It just made me careful not to make the same mistake again.

When I prepare for a race now, I do a few standard things like look at the form and, of course, listen to the trainer. If it's a horse I haven't ridden before, I'll feel him out in the six to eight minutes of the post parade and try to let him gallop away from the lead pony a little. I'll look at his past performances in the *Daily Racing Form* to see if the horse likes to go to the lead or come from off the pace. Julie Krone and Rosemary Homeister, Jr. helped me a lot in handicapping races when I first started riding because I didn't know how to interpret the data in the form. I was so "green." My husband Jerry had to show me the measures (the poles) on the racetrack. When I'm going to the gate, I try to stay focused and calm because the horses feel my feelings before I even know them. Obviously, if my horse is nervous, I try to settle and calm him.

Races unfold in different ways—not always according to plan. As Mr. Jerkens says, "You have to have a plan A and a plan B." Horses have different temperaments on different days, so I have to ride the race as it comes up.

I love riding two year olds, especially first-time starters in short races. I also love riding on the turf because it is so natural for some horses to let go and run on the grass. I've been so lucky to race at Aqueduct, Belmont, and Saratoga in such a short time. I'm looking forward to riding at Gulfstream Park next.

I have to mention Braulio Baeza. To me he was the best jockey ever, and it is so wonderful to have his help in my life. He takes time to go over my races on replay with me, and I am grateful for his continued support. Mike Smith and Julie Knone also spent time to help me. When I was growing up, I admired Steve Cauthen and female jockey Robyn C. Smith.

I don't entertain the thought of injury when I'm racing. In fact, injury crosses my mind more when I'm in my car on the Cross Bronx Expressway in New York than it does when I'm around horses! Driving back and forth to work here at the track is harder than riding in a race on the track. I feel I should wear my racing helmet in the car! My father was very concerned about the injury factor when I became a jockey because he was an orthopedic doctor and had seen so many back injuries in other athletes as well. But he supported me in my decision to be a jockey anyway. He believes in me.

After my first successful meet at Belmont, I was still an apprentice jockey. I didn't know which direction to take for the summer, whether to go to Monmouth Park in New Jersey or Saratoga, knowing that apprentice riders never had ridden a lot at Saratoga in the past and that it was very expensive to live up there. So what did I do? I asked Mr. Jerkens, of course! "Mr. Jerkens, what should I do? Should I stay at home and ride Monmouth Park or try Saratoga?" I asked, perplexed. "Well, is it a money thing?" he asked back. "Well, it's very expensive to live up at Saratoga, and I don't know if I'm going to ride enough to pay my rent up there and pay the mortgage at home," I answered. A second later he said," Well, what if I put you on payroll?" I almost fell off my horse and immediately said, "Of course, I would love to go to Saratoga."

It was interesting how it worked out. I didn't have an agent up there. I worked for Mr. Jerkens on his horses from 6:00 to 9:00 A.M., but if there was a horse with another trainer that I could have a possible mount on, at 7:30 A.M. he would say, "Go see that horse," and when 9:00 A.M. rolled around, he would say, "Go hustle some mounts."

Mr. Jerkens is such a wonderful, flexible man with a huge heart. My husband Jerry is always a huge support for me. In this business, as in any business, there are so many ups and downs. It is so wonderful to have someone there for you everyday to say, "Keep with it. You can do it. Keep going." It really is so important.

I had a great meet at Saratgoa. It was the opportunity of a lifetime for me. I had four wins as an apprentice jockey up there. I won on a horse for Mr. Jerkens named Topsy Ropsy. It was my final win as an apprentice. My next win would make me a journeyman, a full-fledged jockey.

I had the best time up there. I felt like a real celebrity. I hadn't been exposed to that kind of thing before—where people wanted my autograph. I walked into Sears, and I was recognized. I get fan mail now. I like all that stuff. It's great, but my focus is always on my riding. I was so happy to win for Mr. Jerkens. It was the last week of the meet, and I wound up being the leading apprentice jockey. So my apprenticeship was over when I won on a horse named Carson County. It was my first win as a journeyman—no weight or any other type of allowance.

Paula Keim-Bruno

Signing autographs at Saratoga.
Courtesy of the Keim-Bruno family.

Marty Basile, my agent before the Saratoga Meet, really only handles apprentice jockeys. So now that Marty couldn't be my agent anymore, I started to discuss with my husband the possibility of taking over the book as my agent. I wasn't sure what to do, so I asked Mr. Jerkens, of course. It wasn't that I thought Jerry was incapable; it's just that I didn't know how it would be received in the industry for my husband to take my book around.

Well, Jerry Bruno, Jr., my husband, has been very well received. He grew up right around the corner from Monmounth Park, is very knowledgeable about Thoroughbreds, and has a genuine love of the whole industry. And who better could sell me than my husband who believes in me and has from the start! Marty, now my former agent, was amazed at how quickly my apprenticeship was over and how well I did. Topsy Ropsy was my fortieth career win. What a way to end my apprenticeship—on Mr. Jerken's horse at Belmont in a handicap race.

My Words of Wisdom

I would tell girls at ten to thirteen years of age who express an interest in becoming jockeys mainly two things. First, they should make sure that they stay focused on getting an education because they can't be jockeys forever. I sound like my mother saying that! Of course, I want to ride forever, but if someday I can't or make the decision not to, I would like to be able to train horses, and I'm getting that education by riding and watching and listening to the trainers I work for, especially Mr. Jerkens. I'm so fortunate to be around Mr. Jerkens a lot. I learn so much from him because he does things in a different way from most people, and I find myself exploring the "whys." Why is he doing it this way? He knows I want to train horses someday, so he takes the time to show and explain things to me.

Second, I would tell girls to stay physically fit. They have to be incredible athletes to be jockeys. They should start riding as early as possible and do whatever they need to do to be able to ride, whether it's getting money by cleaning out stalls, feeding, and exercising horses on farms or by working at local riding academies. If they have the drive, they can do whatever they put their minds to. If they have the desire, they should follow their dreams—do it.

When I told my mother I wanted to be a jockey, she said, "Paula, you never regret the things in life you do, you regret the things you didn't do, and if you want to do this, we will support you in whatever way we can." My mother has every win photo of me in her office and listens to every race call.

Mind, body and spirit working together are so important—and keeping my attitude right. I focus and center myself. I also tune into the horses. I feel I was gifted as a kid with a lot of opportunities to be around horses and to have so many good experiences with them. I am blessed with my size (4'11") and don't have to worry too much about my weight. Some jockeys do. So I try to eat a balanced diet as any athlete would. I do nothing extreme in my diet or in my fitness routine. It's very important to remember to stay grateful.

My enjoyments outside the track besides my husband are our three dogs: two Jack Russell's named Jack and Jill and a Labrador that is sixteen years old. They are our kids; in fact, they are all going to Florida with us for the upcoming Gulfstream Meet. This was another decision made as a result of asking Mr. Jerkens.

My husband and I never went on a honeymoon after our marriage, but our summer at Saratoga turned out to be the best honeymoon ever. After a workday, Jerry and I went to an early movie or dined out with friends and extended family members. We love watching the replays of the races at night on television, and, of course, we look at the agenda for the next day, including who we want to see about future mounts and workouts in the morning. To sum it up, "I just love being a jockey. I just love it!"

Paula Keim-Bruno

Jill Jellison. *Courtesy of Equi-Photo, Inc.*

Jill Jellison

Although she rode horses in Japan one year and occasionally rides in New York and New Jersey, Jill is happiest and winningest on her home turf—the racetracks of New England. She feels fortunate to have grown up, lived and worked in an area where gender and horse racing have not bucked heads as much as in other parts of the country. It is a comfort to read about Jill's steady career and simple pleasures in life.

Since riding her first horse to a win in 1982, Jill has quietly, without much fanfare, won as many races as other jockeys both male and female at higher-profile racetracks. By 1989 she was the second leading female rider in the country. In 1993 she rode her one thousandth winner, becoming only the fifth woman to do so. By 1996 she had 1,260 wins, 1,234 places, and 1,279 shows to her credit with lifetime winnings of $7,037,035.00 for the horse owners. Jill continues to be happy riding at Suffolk Downs and Rockingham Park where trainers such as Kevin King use only women riders and others such as Bob Raymond provide sound, quality horses to ride daily.

Born to Be a Jockey

I was born in Woonsocket, Rhode Island, on November 22, 1963, to parents Marilyn and Charlie. I have two brothers and one sister. My father always had horses and taught me to ride when I was three years old. By the time I was four years old I was going over to Bob Raymond's Bobcat Stables on Lamoureux Boulevard in North Smithfield everyday. Bob Raymond was like a second father to me and got me started in racing. My brothers and sister don't make it out to the track that often nowadays, but when they do, they scream at the top of their lungs, rooting for me. I like working in the New England area because I can go home and be with my family very easily.

I grew up on a farm and always loved horses. I would ride anybody's horse. Some people would have really tough horses that nobody could ride. I would say to them, "Oh, let me ride him." I got along with almost any kind of horse. I wasn't into Thoroughbreds yet. I rode mostly western style. I had a lot of fun. Bob Raymond trained Thoroughbreds and spent years watching me ride all those crazy horses. He told me he always had it in his mind that when I was old enough I should learn to gallop his Thoroughbreds.

I turned fourteen. I started to gallop Bob's horses. He would say, "I'm gonna make you a jockey." At that age I wasn't even thinking about work. I was just having fun. I was just a kid, I thought. But at sixteen I was bored at school. I kept missing classes to go over to the barn to break horses in the afternoon. I started realizing that I had to do something now to make money. One day

Growing up on a farm
with horses I loved.
Courtesy of the Jellison family.

Bob said to me, "If you are going to be here all the time, I'm going to teach you to be a jockey." I left the Woonsocket school system and devoted my entire time to working on Bob Raymond's farm with his horses.

Not a Typical Teenager

When I was fifteen and sixteen years old, I was leading a totally different life from that of the other kids. Although a great many of my peers rode horses, my dedication to riding was beyond the ordinary. I had one girlfriend, Fran, who rode very well, and we broke horses together on the farm. Socially, I never dated. I had boys as friends. When I was a younger teenager, twelve and thirteen years old, I used to go tree climbing and roof climbing with the neighborhood boys. By the time I was eighteen I wanted to be a jockey big time, Fran didn't, and we went in different directions. I was never really interested in boys, honest to God, until I was twenty years old. I loved the horses, and that was my life. Now that I am thirty-three, I look back and see that I was what people called a "late bloomer." I never went to parties. I hung out at the barn and rode my horses.

Bob Raymond brought me to the racetrack in 1980. I got my exercise license that year. It took a while just to learn to gallop correctly on the track. It was totally different from riding on the farm. The first time I got on a racehorse at the track, he ran away with me for the whole mile. It took me a long time to learn the demeanor of racehorses and the "little tricks" to quiet them or make them gallop nicely. It became a psychological workout besides a physical one.

I didn't consider any other career at that time because I loved the horses. I loved what I was doing. I was galloping the horses, mucking their stalls, rubbing them down and brushing them.

I groomed horses in the three years before riding them at the racetrack. I couldn't gallop horses until I was sixteen at the track. I was still living at home, commuting from Rhode Island to Boston. It was difficult earning my exercise license, I remember, because the trainer I was working for had all these really tough to handle horses. They would all run off in different directions and give me a hard time, but I did it.

I galloped professionally for a good couple of years before I started riding as a jockey. My mom and dad were all for it. Even now, my mom watches all the replays at night. They are as proud of me as they are of my brothers and sister. They don't treat me like a celebrity. My brothers and sister jokingly call me up and say, "Jill, get all the money so we can borrow some." If there are any problems with my nephews, I get a call, "Auntie Jill, can we have . . . ?" They all understand how hard I work, though, and are very supportive—equal work equal pay.

I always felt that once I was on a horse it was equal competition. I think the most difficult part of the job is hustling mounts for a female rider rather than actually riding and competing against the men. I had to prove myself and win races. As long as I'm doing that the trainers and owners will have confidence in me and ride me more and more.

Regarding the issue of a woman's strength compared to a man's strength in controlling a horse, a rider must know when to use a light touch. A lot of horses will respond to a light touch better than to anything else. Sometimes a horse can be "rank," difficult, hard to handle, so by no means can a woman be a skinny little weakling, but she doesn't have to be a man either. Working out by galloping horses in the morning gives me a lot of muscle, really builds me up. I try to eat well, plenty of vegetables and fruit, just like Mom said.

Crossing the finish line on the Bob Raymond–trained Wee Thunder.
Courtesy of Bud Morton.

Jill Jellison

Off the track I'll roller blade a little, mostly for fun and relaxation. I'll work out with weights to strengthen my shoulders and upper arms only if I've been on vacation and am coming back to ride. I'll run on the beach to build up my wind, but as long as I'm racing year-round, I stay quite fit.

When I first began to ride, I watched a couple of older riders, especially Phil Ernest at Suffolk Downs. I noticed how hard he rode, but it never entered my mind that he was a guy and I was a girl so that for me it would be different. The pay is the same. A jockey only gets 10 percent of the horse owner's share of the money if the horse she is on comes in first, second, third, or fourth. My agent gets 25 percent of that money, and I pay my valet who saddles my horses 10 percent of what I make. So I have to work hard, ride a lot, and win a lot of races. I can't let up at all because the minute I do the other jockeys will hustle my mounts.

It's a lot of work for a male or a female. I mostly ride in the New England area and have been treated very fairly, but I know it's tougher in other parts of the country such as California, for instance.

Off to a Great Start

In my first preliminary race I can remember thinking, "Gosh, I'm really tired going into the stretch run, especially in my legs." At that point, of course, I didn't have much experience, and I really wasn't as physically fit as I thought I was. I have to be fit in every part of my body to be able to ride well, so I immediately started running and doing other exercises to build up my legs after that first go around. To qualify for my jockey's license I had to ride two races. As long as a jockey rides straight, the stewards will grant it. Some racetracks don't allow riding with a whip first time out, but at Suffolk Downs they let me. I received my license at eighteen years of age. I was ready for my first professional ride.

I rode a really nice horse, Mighty Peter, my first time out as a licensed apprentice jockey. He was Bob Raymond's best horse, and I don't think in retrospect that I was ready to ride a horse like that. He was a really big, strong horse, and when he came out of the gate, he surged forward. He reminded me of the big, black stallions in the movies. So there I was hanging on, and it took about five strides for me to get a cross on my reins. I had no choice, I just had to let him go. He finished second at 50:1 odds. During the race he brushed another horse, and the jockey on that horse claimed a foul against me. I thought, "Oh, now my first race, and I have a claim against me." But it was not granted, and my position of second place finisher stood.

In racing there are rules as in other sports such as football and baseball; one of them is that a horse must stay straight, and when it does go by another horse, it must stay clean and not go in its path. Sometimes horses bear in and bear out and are difficult to handle and I need all my strength to keep them straight if they have a habit of doing that. When jockeys claim a foul against another jockey, they signal the outrider, the person on the nonracing horse who leads the racehorses onto the track before a race, and the outrider tells the stewards. Nowadays, racetracks have quick official results, and jockeys don't have time to go back to the trainer to explain what happened during the race.

The stewards put up an objection or inquiry sign on the tote board, and then the jockey phones the stewards and says what happened, for instance, "The other horse bumped my horse and knocked me off stride." Then the stewards will review the taped video of the race before making the results official and change the order of finish if they find fault with it. Much to my relief, they didn't find fault with me and Mighty Peter. I actually went on to win four times with Mighty Peter at Finger Lakes Racetrack the following season. He was my first win horse on April 2, 1982.

I rode mostly at Suffolk Downs and Rockingham Park in the years that followed. I was the leading rider at Rockingham Park in 1989 and at that time the second leading female rider in the nation with 220 wins to my credit. I like sticking around New England. If I picked up and went to another track in a different area, it would be almost like starting all over again unless I went with a big outfit that had twenty to thirty horses with them. I've also found quite a few trainers here such as Kevin King who just ride women, meaning they give their horses only to women jockeys to ride. They say it is because they trust the women more than the men.

Honor and Glory

In 1990 I was invited to tour Japan with an all-female riding troupe in the International Queen Jockey Series. I was one of ten jockeys who represented countries such as Canada, New Zealand, and, of course, America. It was a seventeen-day tour that stopped at four different racetracks in Japan. We each received 150,000 yen (approximately 1,000 dollars) for each day we rode plus 5 percent of the purse money for each winning mount. It was a great opportunity and an honor to be one of two female jockeys representing the United States. My American teammate was Lori Young, who rode at Charlestown Racetrack. Of ten girls, I finished second in the series. I also participated in a twelve-girl competition in New Mexico the following year called the New Mexico State Fair Ladies Challenge. Tammi Campbell and I represented the New England area there, but it was everyone for herself. It was a beautiful part of the country to explore and an honor to ride in the competition.

The year 1993 was big for me, especially October 6, 1993, when I rode my thousandth winner, becoming the fifth woman to do so. I guided a horse named Topsy Turn from off the pace in the fourth race at Rockingham Park. I was told I entered elite company with Julie Krone, Patti Cooksey, Vicky Aragon, and Vicky Warhol at the time. I thought I was going to win the thousandth race the Saturday before, but I had trouble in the race. I'm thrilled the win was on one of Bob Raymond's horses. As I walked through the paddock during the days before it happened, and the trainers would yell, "You're going to do it on my horse," but Bob was more emotional when it happened than I was. Bob had thirty-three winners at that meet and I rode all of them, but he was overwhelmed by my thousandth victory. Later that year the New England Turf Writers Association voted me the Lou Smith Award for outstanding yearly achievement.

Jill Jellison

Thrilled by my thousandth win on a horse trained by Bob Raymond. *Courtesy of the Jellison family.*

My lifetime record at the end of 1996 was, 10,064 starts, 1,260 wins, 1,234 places, and 1,279 shows for earnings of $7,037,035.00.

We Are Family

We are like one big family here at the racetrack. Taking nothing away from my mother and father, brothers and sister, and now, nieces and nephews, my horseracing friends and coworkers are my family. I lost contact with most of the kids I went to school with. When I have occasion to meet people outside the racetrack, they usually say to me first thing, "Wow, you're a jockey," and then they say, "Don't you get scared riding those big horses?" So I dated people in the horse industry, not many though, maybe two or three. At the moment, I don't desire a family of my own with kids. A lot of my friends have kids, and it scares me a bit to think of the responsibility. I'll probably grow old by myself and have a few horses. They'll be my kids. I keep to myself a lot. Women jockeys really do get along well with the male jockeys for the most part, contrary to what people think. They tease us occasionally and we tease them, but they say "congratulations" when we win and "good luck" when we are going out on the track and "nice ride" when we come in.

We have had problems with a few male jockeys in the past. Tammi Campbell and I actually got into a fight with one of them. I guess he felt he had to intimidate us. Tammi punched him out one year, and I had to punch him out the next year. I just hit him on the way into the jockeys' clubhouse. I was fined two hundred dollars for it because it happened where everyone could see. The fine would have only been one hundred dollars if I had waited until we were inside. This guy really didn't like girl riders for some reason. But it was worth the fine. He's been nice to us ever since. A couple of others through the years got sarcastic, tough, and called us names if we beat them in a race, but not lately.

I don't lead a wild social life off the track even if I'm out with horse people. I can't do it. We all work so hard, and we have to keep up our strength.

What's on My Mind and What Isn't

Girls who want to be jockeys should get early experience galloping horses on a farm, not at the racetrack. They should take riding lessons earlier than that and make sure they have a true love of horses. When they are old enough (each state differs), they can get jobs on the racetrack, work around the horses, and get to know them and the owners and trainers. Trainers, especially, are not going to put someone without solid riding experience on a horse that's worth a lot of money and is making money. So girls should get out and about as early as possible and keep physically fit.

I've been riding fourteen years now, and as long as I'm riding well, making money, and am happy, I'll keep on riding. I've often wondered why there isn't a retirement age for jockeys, but there isn't. Maybe fifty would be a good age. I've only been injured three times in fourteen years. My worst injury was when I broke my shoulder and dislocated it. I belong to the Jockey's Guild, and they carry insurance for us, so all my medical bills and disability time are paid. I think the average career length for a jockey is thirty years, about the same for other athletes. I don't think about injury when I ride, not at all. I think if I start to think that way it will be time to retire.

I think about winning races and making money. I hate to lose. Sometimes I get double called (named) on two horses in the same race and in making a choice of which horse to ride, it comes down to being loyal to certain trainers who will stick with me, the ones who will not "fire" me if I don't bring a horse in to win every time. He may not be the horse in the race with the best chance in that particular race, but the trainer will ride me again and again on other horses, and next time that horse might be in a perfect spot to win.

I have great fans. People in the press often ask me, "Do men bother you when you ride?" Generally, no. Sometimes I'll hear if I don't win, "Ah, go home and do the dishes," but it's not that bad. We're out there trying, and they know it. I actually think the public gives men jockeys a harder time than women.

Now that I'm starting to get a little older, I think about what I would like to do when I finish my riding years. I definitely would like to have a farm and raise horses in Florida, maybe in Ocala.

When I first started riding, I used to get emotionally overattached to each horse that I rode, but I don't and can't let myself do that anymore. I remember I was on a horse that broke down in the middle of a race. I had to stop and unsaddle him before they put him down. I couldn't stop crying. I was very upset for a long time, but I had to pick myelf up and go on or else just fall apart. It becomes a professional thing to do.

I look forward to riding a lot of horses. I've been around most of them since they were babies. I know their personalities, and some of them, believe it or not, are smarter than the oth-

Jill Jellison

ers. They get to know me, too, and when they see me coming with my helmet and my whip, they know what's coming up. I have one little horse that grabs the whip out of my pocket and swings it all around like he's going to hit me with it.

My job is one of the most difficult jobs a female could possibly have. I believe I should enjoy whatever I choose to do in life and that it's important to stay healthy and happy. I work hard, and it's tough sometimes. Hey, its not easy going out every day and getting dirt in my face. . . . but I love it!

Gwen Jocson. *Courtesy of John Pantalowe, World Wide Racing Photos.*

Gwen Jocson

Dubbed the "Comeback Kid," Gwen had broken all her ribs, her collar bone and sternum, fractured her neck, and had a concussion by the time she was nineteen. She then sustained another fractured neck and other bone injuries while climbing the ranks as a Thoroughbred jockey over the next thirteen years.

Gwen came from a family in which nobody had anything to do with horses. They were shocked when at five years of age she exclaimed, "Mom, I want to be a jockey." Mostly self-taught, she made her way from very humble beginnings in Charleston, South Carolina, to riding for veteran trainers such as Danny Hurtack in Florida. After an invitational riding meet in Peru, Gwen spent a couple of years racking up win after win at New York and Chicago racetracks. When Philadelphia Park Racetrack announced it was opening year-round, Gwen saw this as a golden opportunity to build a name for herself in a specific geographical area. Within four months of her arrival there she was leading rider. By her third anniversary as a licensed jockey she had won 346 races and brought $2,647,882.00 to the horse owners in prize monies. She still rides with steady success in the Philadelphia area.

Southern Beginnings

I was born in Charleston, South Carolina on April 13, 1966. My mom was only eighteen, and my Dad was in his twenties. They divorced when I was nine. When I was five, I saw a horse race on television and said, "Mom, I want to be a jockey." Nobody in my family had anything to do with horses; everyone was shocked when I did. Luckily, we moved to a place in South Carolina with my stepfather when I was thirteen, and the lady across the street had hunters and jumpers. Her name was Bobbie Brostoff. At first I didn't know where the horses were because all I saw was a horse trail and a long, long, winding road. I investigated where the road went and saw the horses and got them to come up to the fence of the property. Then I jumped on them. There were two gray horses, and I didn't know the difference between them because at that age (I was fifteen) I didn't have much horse knowledge. One day I jumped on one, and she walked around the field all nice and calm. Another day, I jumped on a gray horse, thinking it was the same horse, and she took off across the field. I fell off of her, and they found me knocked out because she went through a fence. So I was caught getting on Bobbie's good show horses.

After Bobbie calmed down, she asked if I was scared. "Scared of what?" I said. So she started to let me be around the horses. I cleaned stalls, and she gave me lessons—little did I know she was one of the top instructors on the jumper circuit in America. Her husband was a research scientist for the University of South Carolina; he worked with leukemia and brain diseases. Not too long after that, Bobbie and her husband divorced and the farm went up for sale. My parents scrounged up some money, we were really poor, I mean really poor, and bought me a horse for two hundred dollars. The horse was lame, but I read books and took her out into the field and basically taught myself how to ride. Bobbie was only able to give me lessons for three months.

I started to enter horse shows, small local ones that I could get into for a little money. In three horse shows I won twenty-six ribbons. Everything I had on—the clothes, the tack, the saddle— was borrowed for those shows. Bobbie said I was always very natural on a horse, almost as if I had ridden in another lifetime. I wound up teaching my younger brother, Pattie, to jump horses when he was two years old in our backyard. I also have another brother, Jerry Jocson.

On the Road

I left home when I was seventeen to be with my dad for a little while and then came back to South Carolina. I used to hitchhike with my saddle from where I was living to a Thoroughbred farm to break-in the babies for $3.40 an hour. I was eighteen by then. I saved up enough money to buy a motorcycle and drove that back and forth so I wouldn't have to hitchhike. I did that for about one year, and I met a guy who had a yearling who took me to Aiken, South Carolina, for another year. I came back home. I had $60 and a duffle bag when I bought a bus ticket and went to Florida. I worked on a farm in Davie, Florida. I worked so hard. The people there after about six months lost the farm because of a tax problem, so I went over to Calder Racetrack because it was close by.

I stood by the gate. I didn't know anything about the racetrack. A fellow let me in, and I managed to get a job with Jerry Pace. I didn't think I was good enough to gallop horses at a racetrack, so I walked horses for him. But I soon realized I was a lot better than I thought. Being from a farm, I hadn't compared myself to that many people. I worked around there for a little while, getting hired and fired and hired again. Then I met the assistant for veteran trainer Danny Hurtack. He brought in a real problem horse to work out of the gate. So I worked this horse, and he couldn't believe I got this horse to run. He said, "Come by barn 41, and I'll give you a job!"

I galloped horses for Danny Hurtack for a year. I, of course, still wanted to be a jockey but didn't think I knew enough. One day, Danny walked up to me and asked, "Are you ready to ride a race?" I was taken aback, but said, "Yeah!" What I did know about myself was that I always had a way of communicating with horses through my hands. So one week later I rode my first race (July 18, 1989). My horse wasn't the favorite; he wasn't supposed to win. We won, and the horse paid twenty-five dollars at the betting windows. I rode about thirteen more horses for Danny, and he offered me a contract. I was scared to sign the contract because of what I had heard from other "big" riders about how much money I could make on single mounts and other working restrictions. It was a three-year contract, and I thought that was too long, I didn't want anyone in control of my life but me.

At Calder two gentlemen came up from South America and wanted two girls to come down there and ride. They were paying one thousand dollars plus all the jockey percentages of the winnings. In September I went to Peru. I won on my first horse there and was paid two hundred dollars.

A lot of "first" things stand out in my mind. I seem to have luck with "first" things. I won my first race the first time out. I went to Peru and won on the first horse I got on. When I went to New York, I won the first race there. The first time I rode in an allowance race, I won. The first time I rode in a stakes race, I won. Every time I had a bad accident and was laid up, the first race back, I always won.

We were down in Peru for two weeks. I loved the country. It was like stepping through a time window, stepping back in time to how racing was one hundred years ago. There were lots of people tending to one horse. The food was excellent and the countryside beautiful. Nobody paid attention to traffic lights, and people drove cars with four different size tires on them! It was the experience of a lifetime.

I came back to the States; Danny Hurtack was upset with me for not signing a contract. A friend of mine had a house in New York. I didn't know what to do. I really didn't have enough experience to hustle mounts, and I needed to gallop horses to get some money for basics. I was only making two hundred dollars a week. I had a car with more than two hundred thousand miles on it and holes in the floorboard. So I was basically starving. I hadn't yet won my fifth race. My boyfriend at the time, actually right before I won my first race, was in a car accident and died. I didn't have any ties to anyone, so I thought the best thing to do now was to travel around a bit and educate myself.

Onward and Upward

I went up to stay with my friend in New York. I worked horses at Aqueduct Racetrack. I rode my first race up there at Aqueduct and won. I looked in the newspaper and saw there weren't many "bug" riders. So my friend and I went to my Dad's house in the Chicago area, which we discovered was a two-hour drive away from the track, Sportsman's Park. We had to leave every morning at 3:00 A.M. in the freezing cold to get to work—bone-numbing, freezing cold. Sportsman's Park had to be the coldest racetrack in the world! Nobody knew me, but I was able to get an agent there anyhow. I won my fifth race there, rode a few more races, and then had an accident and broke my neck. I was out for five months. I was able, however, to get back down to South Carolina to have the surgery. When I got back home, the doctors said it was a lot worse than they had originally thought. They told me I would never ride again, would be lucky if I could walk again, and would never be able to use my left arm for anything. I didn't want to have surgery after hearing all that; my mother nearly had to blackmail me into having the ten and one-half hour surgery.

I did have the operation and shortly after went back down to Florida to recuperate. I could walk. I started galloping horses again but couldn't open or close my left hand. I would hold my left hand closed around the reins by putting my right hand around it. I got back on the track

Given Jocson

Crossing the finish line on Fox Foot Ginny at Sportsman's Park after a 3:00 A.M. wake-up call. *Courtesy of Luongo Photo.*

FOX FOOT GINNY

JAMES J. O'TOOLE   OWNER
JAMES J. O'TOOLE   TRAINER
GWEN JOCSON   JOCKEY
COPYRIGHT 1990 LUONGO PHOTO

1:43:0   1 MILE

WINDY JULIE 2ND
WAY TO SAY 3RD
$7,000 PURSE
APRIL 8, 1990

SPORTSMAN'S PARK

and went back up to Hawthorne Racetrack in the Chicago area and won three more races but not without incident. The first horse I rode coming back from my injury collapsed at the finish line from a heart attack; I had to go back to the hospital and get checked out. The second horse I rode broke a leg at the quarter pole, and I went down again.

I started to look in the newspaper to see which other tracks were opening up. I saw that Philadelphia Park was opening, and it was going to be their first year as a year-round racetrack. Garden State Park also was opening in New Jersey. My friend who I was traveling with in those days wanted to go to Garden State; I wanted to go to Philadelphia. So we left the Chicago area. I sat out the winter in Philadelphia, and in January when the track started defrosting, I started riding. By April I was leading rider.

I rode a lot of long shots and won. When I took a call on a horse in the morning, I didn't know if it was going to be a long shot or not—that was someone else's opinion. Lots of times I'll

Pam Kelber and I standing by the scale used to confirm the total weight allowance the winning horse carried in the race. *Courtesy of Luongo Photo.*

get on a horse in the morning that seems sound and is working well and when I get to the track it is on the tote board at 20:1 and it wins. I don't think trainers discriminate by giving long shots only to the girl riders. A girl who shows talent, aggression, and a personality for the racetrack will get mounts; a trainer won't discriminate between her and a male jockey. I see some girls come to the racetrack with their nails done perfectly and lipstick on, and I'm not saying that's a bad thing, but some of the trainers won't take them seriously. They look like they are going to a beauty contest instead of to work. You can dress nicely, dress well, but be ready to work.

I really didn't have to convince people that I was serious about riding, even when I was younger. My mom and stepfather always supported me in finding a way to do what I wanted. When I told my mother I wanted to be a jockey, she didn't say, "Well there isn't a racetrack in South Carolina, so you can't think like that." She said, "Well, work hard and find a way to do it." She always pushed me to learn for myself. Even when I would ask her, "What's the telephone number for so and so," she would say, "There's the phone book, look it up." So when I decided to be a jockey, I didn't expect anyone to hold my hand and show me how to do it. I found out how to do it and made my own connections. I learned not to lean on anyone from my mother. She's very independent. She's led a hard life and survived.

Besides my mother, my other role models were, for one, Bobbie Brostoff. She was a very wealthy woman. I had never known what wealthy was. I would see *Miami Vice* on TV and say,

Gwen Jocson

"Yeah, right!" Even watching *Laverne and Shirley*, I thought people lived like that just on TV. I had never seen the outside world as a young kid. Bobbie took me to plays; she showed me lots of things. Most of the girls in my family married very young; my mom is the twelvth of twelve children. I had six girl cousins born the same year I was, and they all have children already. They each had a child by the time they were eighteen. Nobody really thought of going to college. I did have two uncles who went into their own business, but Bobbie showed me that someone could be rich, could buy a house, could go to nice places, and own jewelry and nice clothes. I didn't know as a kid about going skiing, going on vacation.

In racing I didn't have just one particular role model. Mr. Pierce, Danny Hurtack's assistant trainer, helped me a lot. He watched me ride, and when I worked horses for him, if I dropped my stick I had to pay him twenty dollars. I have a lot of respect for that man. There was always help at the racetrack to learn more; I just had to ask. Jockeys Bobby Colton and Mario Verge helped me. Julie Krone took me under her wing, not only about racing but as a person. After one of my injuries, during my recovery period, she came and dragged me out of the house, took me dancing, befriended me. When we got to talking a lot, I found her life mirrored mine. She worked hard, did it on her own, got herself where she wanted to be. I admire her a lot; she has the ability to stick it out when times get tough. I'm also still amazed as I look at my mom now.

When I was younger, my peers were mostly my family with all the cousins. I had very few friends outside the family. I didn't verbalize too much to them about being a jockey, but I rode everything; I tried to turn everything into a horse. I read every single book in the library on horses. I daydreamed about riding constantly. Our family did a lot of fishing, and I swam in the river a lot. I pay a lot of money now for seafood. When I grew up, it was free and plentiful; it's a hard thing to do.

When my career took off, I had a new large family, my racetrack family. I didn't have enough time or stayed long enough in one place to acquire a lot of new friends. The most outside contact I had was with journalists, and they would ask questions like "Do you own the horses you ride? Do you ride the same horses all the time? How much do you weigh? Do you have to gain or lose weight to ride certain races?" It made me realize how little people outside the racetrack really know about the industry and how nice it would be to educate them.

I'm a natural lightweight, but some jockeys have to work hard at it. I think one of the problems for teenagers who want to ride is that when they try to ride professionally at sixteen years of age because they think they are going to be too big in a couple of years, it puts them in double jeopardy. One, they are going to have no education if and when they get too big or wind up not riding, and it's very hard to go back to school after living this lifestyle. Two, if they are lightweight at sixteen and naturally start to fill out by the time they are eighteen, they wind up starving themselves and putting themselves at risk all around. So I say they should finish school. When they are eighteen, they are not "behind" if they are indeed going to be good riders, good jockeys. If they eat right, stay fit, and take care of themselves, they can make the proper decisions. I don't think there is a lot of anorexia or bulimia in this industry because those disorders are about people thinking they should look a certain way. Jockeys aren't concerned about looking good. A jockey who is currently a jockey is not more than 120 lbs. Jockeys are small in stature and usually can take two or three pounds off easily. A jockey can't be anorexic or bulimic and have the strength to ride five and six races a day. Jockeys are hard as rocks in muscle tone, so anyone out there who thinks there is rampant anorexia or bulimia in horse racing is misinformed.

I don't think jockeys are of any one nationality either. It seems to be regional. In Miami there are a lot of Spanish-speaking jockeys, more so than up north. But up north there are a lot more female jockeys, and I don't know exactly why.

When girls come up to me and ask me what they should do to become jockeys, I tell them find a place that has riding horses, meet people, and go that route. They should eat right, stay fit, get an education. Riding is a seven-day-a-week lifestyle; it will become their life. The younger girls are more concerned with the horse than I am, but they will ask if I have a favorite horse or what happens when a horse has an accident.

I try not to become emotionally over involved with the horses, but horses have different personalities, and I do feel things about them. I rode a horse once that broke down in the middle of the race, and when I had to get off her, I stood on the track and cried. She was a horse that always tried and gave it her all. Some horses are "rats" in personality; they know what they can do, and they don't even try. But some have real heart. A horse named Amberfax was probably my favorite. He was a goofy horse that nobody got along with but me, and he was a strange horse to ride. But he always tried and stands out in my memory. I didn't win a lot of races with him, but he was a real hard-knocker. I rode him over a three-year period.

Sometimes I am assigned to ride a horse that I have never been on, not even in the morning workouts, and sometimes I ride horses over and over again. I get to know all their little quirks and likes when I ride them more than two or three times. With some horses I say to myself, "Oh no, I have to ride that crazy horse again!" But I figure out a way every time. It's like any job; I may not particularly like dealing with some parts. If the horse were the only thing I had to deal with, it would be easy, but I have to deal with the trainer, the owners, the owner's friends, and commentators who write, "Rider change improves this horse," when I rode the horse the last time!

A lot of things go into how a jockey rides a race. Mostly, I listen to the trainer's directions or the owner's comments on what the horse likes or doesn't like. A jockey may want to ride the horse entirely differently from the instructions, so it's not that easy to please the "boss" and to make decisions as the race unfolds about how to give that horse the best ride. Some horses can't even be tapped with a stick; they will pin their ears back and stop. So horses have different temperaments on different days and no one can always anticipate their little quirks.

Horse racing is a very honest sport. Jockeys don't pull back or not try on horses. If a horse takes a misstep or starts to act funny during a race, the jockey can tell right away and will act in a manner that is safest for the horse and all the other horses and jockeys in the race. As for the notion of race fixing, there are usually ten horses in a race, which means there are ten different trainers,

Given Jocson

ten different owners, and ten different jockeys. Who would want to take the back seat? Jockeys at the smaller tracks are out there trying to win every race they can, and jockeys at the big tracks ride for larger purse money and don't need to concern themselves with impossible strategies. Plus, there are stewards and cameras. The races are video-taped from three different angles and filed. Would a horse listen if a jockey suddenly went out to the track and said, "Hey, Mr. Blue Stockings, just don't run today"?

The Comebacks

I'm one of the few jockeys who really talks about her injuries. I'll go into the jock's room and say, "Oh, remember when I broke this or fell and this happened?" and they all will say, "Oh God, don't talk about that!" And I'll say, "What?" I've watched every one of my spills. The last spill I had was really bad. If I were watching that on replay and didn't know it was me, I would say, "That person has to be dead." My horse went down, and I got run over by another horse. I cracked my ribs. I have a phobia about hospitals. Unless I'm very badly injured, no one can keep me there. But people should know that more than 90 percent of our injuries are not critical. It is very rare that anyone is paralyzed or dies. I've ridden more than six thousand races and have only been badly hurt twice. Most horse riders will have a broken bone in their lifetimes. I'm kind of proud of my injuries; they are like battle scars. Jockeys are such fit athletes that they can ride until way into their fifties. There is no mandatory retirement age. Some of the female jockeys have left racing to have families but have come back because they love the sport and missed racing.

Financially, jockeys are paid a standard fee of only thirty-five dollars a mount unless they win, place, show, or come in fourth—then they get 10 percent of the horseowner's share. The government takes 33 percent of that share, and the jockeys have to pay agents and valets. So when people say, "Ah, that jockey didn't try on that horse," it is ridiculous.

When I broke my neck, twice in fact, I had a hard time getting trainers and owners to ride me again. Even though they liked me and the public liked me, they were afraid that if I got hurt again on their horses, it would be bad publicity—"Jock's career over on my horse." I had to fight and come back against all that. I have no fear about getting back on a horse; I have no fear about anything. If I don't think a horse is right, I'll say something and just won't ride him, not because I'm afraid to ride him but because I don't want to see his career ended. Horses have comebacks too, especially after they have been freshened up away from the track for a while.

Woman make excellent exercise riders. If girls want to be jockeys, they should not let anything stand in their way. There are lots of jobs with horses, good jobs. If young girls take riding lessons, go to a racetrack, reach out, come to the jock's room, write a letter, someone will help them. They should educate themselves, read the *Daily Racing Form,* and get acquainted with who's who. They must be prepared to work very hard. There isn't a lot of back-patting in this industry when someone first starts out. Nobody says, "Oh, you really cleaned that stall well." They are just expected to do it right.

Great Women in the Sport of Kings

I never want to be poor again. I never want to have to buy generic brand food at the supermarket. I like going out to a restaurant and ordering exactly what I would like. When I first started to win, I went out and bought all new furniture. I came home everyday and just looked at it and touched it. I always said as a kid that I would buy my mother a car if I ever won the lottery or made a lot of money. She had always driven old, broken-down ones, so when I started making money riding, I bought her a new car and paid cash for it.

Into the Future

I want to ride for as long as I can, but I know it's impractical to think I can ride much past my fifties, so I'm hoping to make a transition into another part of the horse-racing industry. I can't imagine ever working with people other than racetrack people or a life without horses. Maybe I'll pin-hook (buy and sell horses) or become a trainer. I find that the more I learn, the more I have to learn. I'd really like to buy and sell horses, condition, and race them. I would meet people in other areas of horse racing and get to travel a lot; I like that. I have the best people to turn to for advice, and I feel I have a really good eye for a horse. When I was off from racing for two years, I bought a yearling for five thousand dollars, conditioned him, and sold him for twenty thousand dollars, so I feel I can self-educate myself a little more and do it well someday. Bobby Colton did a survey once and found that 25 percent of the jockeys made 75 percent of the money and 75 percent of the jockeys made 25 percent of the money, so it's a lot of work just to make a living. I have to be dedicated.

One of my more relaxing moments. One day I would like to meet the right person and have a family of my own, including lots of animals. *Courtesy of Gwen Jocson.*

Gwen Jocson

When I'm not racing, I'm fishing in the canals and deep sea fishing. I love to snow ski. I cook. I love to shop. I write poetry. I watch movies and hang out with my friends although I don't have a lot of free time. I go out dancing; I love to dance. I read a lot, especially about bloodlines of horses and what's going on at other tracks around the country. When I socialize, I mostly socialize with other jockeys. Most of the male jockeys are married, so I get to know their wives too.

Male jockeys never gave me a hard time on or off the track. I think people treat me the way I let them treat me. If I demand respect, I'm going to get it, and if I act like a wimp, I'm going to be treated like a wimp. I have an agent now, but I find the jockeys that do the best are also able to sell themselves and have personalities. They are able to establish relationships with the owners and the trainers and always find something positive to say about the horses they ride even if they finish last. One day the horse is going to be better placed in a race and win, and the owner or trainer may have other horses for the jockey to ride.

The racetrack pays jockeys, so they don't have to chase their money around. When the horse makes money, the track puts it into an account and dispenses it.

I get a lot of fan mail. I went down to Jockey Day at the OTB. I think it's really important to do things like that. Anybody who asks me for a photo or an autograph, always gets it. The racing fans support the industry.

Left, me in my crazy Halloween punk wig; *center,* Steve Pegano a friend who is also steward at the racetrack, and *right,* Karla Ranbarran, the first female jockey in Trinidad. *Courtesy of Gwen Jocson.*

Great Women in the Sport of Kings

Because I come from a large family, I would like to meet the right person someday and have my own family, but I can't just go out "shopping" for a husband. He would have to understand my lifestyle. I'm very independent, but I don't feel women have to choose either a career or a family. They can do both. I was engaged once, but it didn't work out, and he was in the racing industry. So it just has to be right.

When I go home now to my family in South Carolina, they don't treat me like a celebrity, they're just amazed at how fast I can eat!

A Tribute from Karla Rambarran

I became the first girl to ride in Trinidad in 1983 and rode with fair success until I came to America in 1992.

Being a girl jockey in America is not easy. God knows I tried, but I couldn't do it. I admire these girls a lot, not only because they can ride as well or better than most of the guys (who, by the way, get the better breaks), but they do it day and night, year after year. Boy, they should be awarded for stamina.

Race riding isn't easy; for girls it's almost impossible. They still have a lot of voices against them. "She's weak. She's scared. She's not aggressive enough." It is surprising how biased so many people are.

It's not only the fact that girls have to control an animal that weighs about one thousand pounds at speeds of approximately 40 mph; oh, no, that's not the half of it. Dealing with trainers and owners who like to make their lives miserable is another aspect, and, of course, the competition is fierce. In fact, it's surprising how many guys don't make it.

What can I say about Gwen? I don't think anyone in racing has broken more bones (her neck twice, shoulders, ribs, legs, everything) and made more successful comebacks. But for some reason these things don't bother her when she's riding again. Gwen not only comes back, she wins and wins and wins. Maybe her bones aren't there, but no one has a bigger heart or can be a more aggressive race rider. How she gets there everyday, smiling and going on, I don't know.

From Gwen Jocson

I'm very happy and very proud to be a part of this book. I think I've had a wonderful life and have a wonderful family. The people I have reached out and touched and who have touched me in my life with racing and whatever else I've done have just amazed me. I've had great opportunities and have gotten to travel and meet people. I've had a very happy life, and I hope it continues that way in many different respects.

Gwen Jocson

Darci Rice. *Courtesy of Scooter Davidson.*

Darci Rice

Darci has been sports oriented ever since she can remember and been known to everyone as an outdoor girl full of accomplishments. Although she had a supportive family who were involved with horses and had won many blue ribbons for barrel racing in her younger years, she was on her way to becoming an unhappy chiropractor when her best friend stepped in and reminded her of her greatest happiness in life—horses.

Darci made her career decision and found herself working as an assistant trainer and exercise rider with "jockey" always in the back of her mind. On a trip to California with an Arabian horse outfit in 1992 she was asked to get her jockey's license to ride a particular problem horse. Within one year Darci was back in Delaware riding for Terri Griffith, the leading trainer there. She did so well her riding caught the eye of Jonathan Sheppard, who almost exclusively trains graded stakes winning horses. Since 1993 Darci has spent 99 percent of her career time riding exclusively for Jonathan Sheppard, and he has put her on 99 percent of his horses—commitments not seen anywhere else in modern racing by either trainers or jockeys.

It Was Ridden in the Stars

I was born in Moline, Illinois, on February 19, 1965. My favorite color is orange, bright, brilliant orange. I'm right on the cusp of Aquarius and Pisces; I'm a little of both. When I read my horoscope, I ask, "Which day fits me?" My mom was an astrologer. I have two older sisters, and we are all approximately three years apart. We are a very close family. My older sister, Deann, is very beautiful; in fact, she was a model. She's married now with three children. I'm very similar to my middle sister, Dawn; she's very active with horses. She is a Quarter Horse and show horse trainer. I am very proud of her, and she is very proud of me. I first learned about horses from this sister. When we were little, she always wanted a horse. When she got her first horse, I got my first pony, and we just went from there. My parents always supported all of us in whatever we wanted to do. As long as we were happy and staying out of trouble, they were happy, too. I spent a lot of time with my dad outside. We went hunting, and he let me drive his truck; I could barely reach the pedals. I was only nine or ten. I raced motorcycles at that age, too.

I had a lot of injuries when I was a kid. I was in a very bad go-kart accident that nearly took my life. I fractured my skull and had several hundred stitches. If I did anything bad, I always got caught because I told on myself. I gave enough hints until I got caught. I never skipped school. I don't have any complaints about my childhood. Most people I've met are happy where they are right now as adults. I would rather go back to my childhood; they were the happiest years of my life.

Happy and staying out of trouble with my first pony. *Courtesy of the Rice family.*

My parents divorced when I was older; it was very devastating to me. I was a freshman in college and out of the house, but it was hard then and still is now. To this day I have hopes and dreams that someday they will be together even though they both are remarried. My dad is going through his second divorce. My oldest sister is also divorced now from her first husband, Dave, a harness horse driver I introduced to my family. My dad owned and raced harness horses when I was growing up. I spent all my time at the track with the horses. People at the racetrack would refer to my soon-to-be brother-in-law and me as, "the two blondes." Dave is one of the top drivers in the country, very successful. I was jealous at first of my sister and Dave, but when I realized he was going to become part of the family, I loved him even more. It wasn't as if she were taking him away from me; I wasn't losing a sister, I was gaining a brother. Their marriage broke up around the same time that my parents divorced, and it was very hard on me. I guess I'm a little traditional in that I like things to be the way they are and always were.

I learned from my family's situations that I should be happy for other people in what they decide to do with their lives and not feel it is such a personal issue toward me. If they're happy in their decisions, I'm happy. My middle sister is happily married and has two children. We all try to stay as close as we can.

My Rivals, My Friends

I try hard to get along with people I compete against. I'm not an easy person to get along with in this arena. I'm very competitive on the track, and people expect my calm, laid-back demeanor off the track to carry through once things get going and are taken aback when it doesn't. I seem like two different people. Those whom I know only in competition never get to see the other side of me. I've been told I come off as "stand offish," but it's just that I'm very shy and it's hard for me to get to know people and even harder for them to get to know me. I keep a distance, and sometimes it makes me sad when I'm like that because I expect people to be able to see through it when I don't even give them a chance. Most people tell me that when they initially met me they didn't like me, but after they got to know me and understood me a little better, they liked me. I've been accused of being stuck-up, but I would rather sit and listen than join in until I get to know somebody or a situation.

I went to college on a softball scholarship at Southern Illinois University. That's why I went to college. I was having a hard time with depression and anxiety after I finished college with a bachelors degree in exercise science. I was headed back to school with only a few more years to become a chiropractor and at the same time working in the family business. I felt this wasn't enough, this wasn't it.

My best friend from high school, Paige, turned things around for me. She sat me down and asked me, "Do you remember the last time you were happy?" and I said, "No, I can't remember being happy." I was very depressed saying this. She said, "Come on, think about it, when was the last time

At college on a softball scholarship before my love of horses won out.
Courtesy of the Rice family.

Darci Rice

you were really, really happy?" I had to think about it. I sat there, and she said, "What about when you used to ride your horses, how did you feel then?" I used to barrel race when I was younger, and she reminded me about that. I realized something at that moment and said, "That . . . was the last time I can remember being really happy." I knew at that very moment what I had to do to get my life together.

Back on Track

One day I was sitting in my cousin's office. I was working there in the receiving department. He had all these "win" photos of Thoroughbreds that he owned up on the wall, and he walked in and saw me looking at them. My dad and he were close; in fact, my dad nursed him through some really hard times. I was admiring one horse in particular that had won the Arkansas Derby. My cousin was sort of complaining about how much he had paid for the horse and started to tell me about a little horse someone had given him. He said, "Why don't you buy this horse from me and use it as a barrel horse?" I was very insulted. It was a slam for him to say that because I was a very successful barrel racer. I went back to my desk. I thought to myself, I'm going to get into the Thoroughbred business and someday ride against his horses and beat them! I picked up the phone right at that desk and within three days I had a galloping job at a farm. I was inspired and felt a bit of revenge at the same time. When I think about it in retrospect, I don't think what happened was a bad thing. Maybe my cousin said that to spark me, a little reverse psychology. I went for it.

I was in my early twenties by then, galloping on a farm in Iowa. Jim Bader, who owned the farm, remembered me from barrel racing and decided to give me a shot even though at first he said he didn't need any extra help. I did that for about one year. At this point I had only been to the racetrack to watch, never on the backside.

I got a little sidetracked by going into business with my aunt, who moved me to Florida. She took me for ten thousand dollars, which wiped me out. So I went back to my horses again, started galloping, and never looked back.

I got a job on a farm in Florida. I was in St. Petersburg at the time, so I went to Tampa and Ocala and started knocking on doors on the horse farms. I didn't know a soul and had no contacts. I found a job on a farm where I could both work and live. I worked there for quite a while, galloping and fixing fences and doing any other work that needed to be done.

I was happy just to be working with the horses. My only thought of being a jockey at this point was the memory of watching the Kentucky Derby on television when I was younger and wanting to ride in it. I still believed that I was too tall, almost 5'6," and too heavy. I didn't realize you could do whatever you wanted to if you put your mind to it. I loved barrel racing, the speed and competition, when I was between nine and fourteen years of age. In barrel racing the horse and rider weave around three barrels in a cloverleaf pattern in a timed event. A lot of strategy is involved, and I had to be "in sync" with my horse. I represented Illinois for two years on the youth team at the Quarter Horse Congress, which includes all the top horses and riders in the country.

Barrel racing for the state of Illinois at the national level, bringing home ribbons and money. The techniques and strategies I used then help me now in my Thoroughbred racing career. *Courtesy of the Rice family.*

I was very successful and went all over the country to compete. I was awarded ribbons and money, which went to my parents because I was very involved in sports in high school. If I had personally kept the money, I would have been classified as a professional. We eventually got another horse and in the summer traveled as a family in a motor home, following the circuit. It was great fun and one of the happiest times in my life.

It is no wonder I was depressed after college. The only time I ever saw horses in college was when some buddies and I went out in the middle of the night and rounded up horses at the local state park. I bridled them with hay string, and we rode them in the pastures.

A Work in Progress

I was about twenty-four years old when I worked at the farm in Tampa. Looking back, I see I was in a progression the whole time. I started to gallop the horses on the racetrack. This was a big thing for me. I met a woman who brought me up to Delaware for the summer to take care of some horses. It was a very short-lived thing. She took her horses back to Florida, but I decided to stay in Delaware and did freelance galloping and other work to make money. I came back down to Florida and had a good winter. I met more people, had a lot of support, and was always very, very eager to learn! Only a few people knew that in the back of my mind I wanted to be a jockey, but I still thought I wasn't small enough and good enough. I was too shy to talk with others about it.

Even though I had a lot of support, I was always afraid of failure. I never let anyone know things such as wanting to ride as a jockey, so, therefore, I wouldn't fail at it. I was afraid to say, "I

Darci Rice

want to be a jockey," for fear that people would say, "No," or laugh at me and say, "You'll never make it; you're not good enough!"

Next, I went to California with an Arabian horse outfit that I knew from Delaware. We went out there for the winter. One horse was a problem, and I rode (galloped) this horse better than anyone. When it came time for this horse to race, the woman in charge asked me to get my jockey's license so I could ride Valours Golly Gee. I really liked and got along with her. I didn't go out to California with the intention of furthering my riding, but once they asked, I saw my opportunity and went for it. I still didn't think I was good enough. I got my jockey's license and won my first race out there in January 1992.

I didn't win on Valours Golly Gee the first time I rode her. She was in a race against the boys, a bad spot; it was just to give her a race. The owners reentered her immediately but weren't certain of my abilities. Because I worked full time for the trainer and didn't want to cause conflict, I told them I wouldn't ride the horse even though I was named on her. I didn't want the trainer to lose a client over it. Another jockey named Kami got the mount. Even though I straightened that horse out and ran a race and ran it well, I gave up the chance to ride her that time out. She won the race easily and I had to sit and watch. Kami came into the jockey's room and cried and felt so terrible for me because I had had to sit there and watch the win after I had worked the horse so hard to get there. She would have been my first winner.

The horse on which I did win my first race was also an Arabian, Keen Edge. I wound up winning a total of eleven races on him. My first win came about three weeks after I missed the opportunity on Valours Golly Gee. I still didn't think of myself as a jockey. I was an assistant trainer and worked in the mornings. I rode the horses in the afternoon that neither of the two jockeys who were with the barn wanted to ride.

From California I traveled to Tampa, Florida, with the same outfit for a couple of months. I won my fifth race there on the same horse I won my first race on. My "bug" was ticking. A "bug," or apprenticeship, is either one year or thirty-five wins, whichever is reached last. I went to Delaware for two months just as an assistant trainer, which delayed my "bug." I didn't like that. Regardless, my career was in motion. Things fell into hand, into place. It seemed my career was progressing faster than I was. I couldn't reach my goals quickly enough. Even a bout with vertigo and internal bleeding from a spill didn't keep me away from riding for long.

Terri Griffith was the leading trainer at Delaware Park and started to give me good horses to ride. I did really well. Then I hooked up with Jonathan Sheppard, and he's taken me as far as I am today. Jonathan trains so many great horses. I spend most of my time working really hard with his horses, and he rewards me by giving me great mounts in great races. I know his horses so well because I spend so much time in his barn. I've spent 99 percent of my time for the last four years of my career there. He mostly trains off his farm in Pennsylvania and stables at Delaware Park. In the winter he sends a small string of horses to Florida and moves his basic training operation to Camden in the Carolinas. His forte used to be long races on the turf, but he has a more versa-

64

Winning on a Jonathan
Sheppard–trained horse—
one of my greatest pleasures.
Courtesy of Double J. Photo.

tile group of horses now, dirt horses and sprinters. I think what makes Jonathan and me so successful is that we work as a team. He helps me, I help him. I know his horses, they know me. I know what he expects from his horses and the rider. I do ride occasionally for other trainers, and there are some horses in his barn that I just don't fit, but all in all it's a great relationship.

Somehow fate just steps in to determine my course. I'll luck out and get to ride a horse that suddenly has an open mount, and I'll win. But I always do my best, no matter whom I'm working for. I have a lot of compassion for the animals, and a lot of the trainers realize that. I am living my dream before I dream it almost! Two years ago it was a dream for me just to see Saratoga; now I'm riding stakes races there.

I mainly work in Delaware, Philadelphia, and the Maryland areas unless Jonathan needs me somewhere else, and then I'll fly in for a race. He rides other "big name" jockeys on some of his horses at the bigger tracks. I always thought that was a "catch 22" for jockeys. They can't be big name riders until they ride the good horses, and they can't ride the good horses until they're big name riders.

Darci Rice

But I did all right this year. I got a really nice horse to ride named Powder Bowl. I won the biggest race of my life on her, and it also was the biggest paramutual win for Jonathan. The horse paid $101 to win at the betting windows, and we beat two of the best horses in the country, who were going for records.

My family really doesn't keep up with horse racing that much nowadays, so they don't realize the extent of my success. They got a little taste of it, especially my mother last summer, because people would run up to me and ask me for my autograph.

I have a big fan club at the Atlantic City Racecourse. It's a small track, but I do very well there. The fans really make me feel at home. It's one of the friendliest tracks in the country, and I love that it's by the ocean. I always feel revived when I get near the water; I don't understand it, but it happens every time. I do really well at Tampa Racetrack by the water in Florida, too.

I love to water-ski. I love boating; I do as much as I can. I lie out in the sun a lot. I love being outdoors. When I was growing up, my family went on vacations snow skiing, so I can still do that. I was very athletic always. I love to dance and have fun. I love to laugh and be happy.

I stay fit by riding morning, noon, and night. I think about biking and running, but I don't get a lot of that done nowadays. I'm getting into vitamins and minerals more. I do aromatherapy for "mind food." I've always had a poor appetite. I'm on the road so much that I often don't pay enough attention to my diet. I know I could improve my mind and body, so I am reading up on what would be right for me.

The turf season is my busiest time of the year. It extends from April until November. I keep my nose to the grindstone and just keep going. I'll work the mornings in Delaware, "wherever" in the afternoon, and New Jersey at night, so I get ragged sometimes. I owe it to my body to look into some healthy nutritional supplements.

Some Things Remain the Same

I've always been sports oriented; I grew up with it. When I was in fifth grade I went out for the boys' basketball team. I was the first female to do that. It just wasn't allowed. Actually, they changed the rules in the school system after we—my family backed me—took it as far as we could. A few other girls and their families were with us, also. I was the only girl to play on the boys' Little League team, and I was allowed to do that.

I've found similar resistance to being a female jockey. I think it stems from the old thinking that boys are better than girls at sports. I say and think that "anything they (boys) can do, I can do better." Strength doesn't always count on a horse; it's more of a finesse, a feeling, anyway. Some horses need different kinds of riders. Girl riders differ from one another. Some horses respond to a hand ride; some need to be encouraged by a whip. Whether it's a girl rider or a boy rider who rides the same way, we all weigh about the same. Pound for pound, how much stronger can anyone really be than another?

Put two boy wrestlers who weigh ninety-eight pounds each in the ring, and it's not the one who's stronger who wins, it's the one who knows how to wrestle better. The same is true in racing. Some girls are very aggressive; some aren't. Being nonaggressive is not a bad thing. A smart, thinking rider will make the right moves at the right time and give the horse the encouragement it needs. A good rider will be able to adjust individual style to a horse.

I ride horse by horse. Before a race I like to clear my head and become open to what I can feel through the horse. I try to block everything else out and just get whatever I can from the horse. I always say a prayer for my horse, myself, and all the other riders and horses in the race to be safe, sound, and unharmed. After that, as far as I am concerned, it's all in God's hands. There is a reason for everything. I can't understand why I can't win all the time, but I guess there's a reason behind it!

My goals are to continue doing what I'm doing. Knowing that the winter months are slower for me, I look forward to the spring in Delaware and my turf riding. I don't take to the cold weather too much anymore, so I like to be where it's warm. I don't plan too far ahead; I take each day as it comes.

I've been very fortunate not to have had serious injuries. I've had broken bones like everyone else, but I walked away from two spills last summer almost unharmed. I think I have a very special angel sitting on my shoulder who has done something that deserves some big wings and that's why she's stuck with me. It's a hard job for her to keep me safe. I don't dwell on the possibility that I'm going to be seriously injured. If it's my time, it's my time whether I'm riding a horse or walking across the street or driving a car. Accidents happen all the time. Freak accidents happen. Often I feel safer on a horse than in a car. The risk factor, the challenge in horse racing, actually excites me; it drives me. I would jump off the highest building if I knew I could get away with it. I'm a risk taker. If somebody jumps so far, I want to jump farther, as long as it's my decision. If someone is forcing me, well, that's another matter; I become resistant.

I live very much by my intuition. I consider myself to have a very old soul. It may sound strange, but there are too many things I know about that I have never experienced. In one instance, I refused to ride a horse one time for no good reason, just because my intuition told me not to. He ran the race, broke his leg, and went down. This was early in my career, and I had no knowledge to back up such a decision. It was just a feeling; it's only happened once in my racing career.

When I'm out on the track, I don't think about any of that. I get "plan A, B, C, and D" either from my instructions by the trainers and owners or from my prior experience with the horse. More often than not, most plans fail as soon as the gates open, and I just have to ride the race as it comes up. I can have an idea in my head and study the form all I want, but horses are animals, not machines. If I am in a position where I have to stop and think, it's already too late; it's got to come naturally. I've tried so hard to make the people I work for happy by riding "their" races instead of my own, and it never works out very well. I'm either a hero or a piece of crap at the end of every race I ride!

Dara Rice

67

I've been so wrapped up in my career, so job oriented for such a long time, that I've almost forgotten how to live.Recently, I went through one of the hardest summers emotionally, yet the best businesswise. I found myself putting things down deep so they wouldn't affect my riding, and they didn't. But now that the slower times are here, everything I've put off dealing with is coming up all at once, and it's hard for me.

I would like people to know that maybe a hard shell is covering me, but a soft human is in there somewhere. There is, I know. I have a lot of friends and acquaintances but very few people I've "let in." It's great to be able to turn and talk to somebody whom I really know. I just have myself. My dog Tess, my best friend, died. It has been the hardest thing for me. We were together for eleven years. She was everything to me—my best friend, my spouse, my confidant—and to lose that, well, she was my everything. I had a bridge put in my mouth right before she died. The dentist told me they now do tooth tattoos. Immediately, I thought of my dog, so I have her name, Tess, engraved on my tooth. A constant reminder, she was always there for me, and now that she's not, I feel lost a lot. It's hard sometimes to keep pressing on, but somehow I keep finding the energy to do it.

I love my job. I have a very competitive spirit. My business means everything to me now. Years back, someone very close to me said, "You'll never be as good as you think you are," and that killed me. It broke my spirit. Now I think I go overboard, I overcompensate, I'm very critical of my own performance. I beat myself up more than anybody could.

When I win, people say they don't see much difference from when I lose. They say I don't care, that I don't enjoy it, and that I take it for granted. But that's not true. I'm too afraid to show how happy I am because I don't want it to be taken as being overconfident or cocky. I try to stay on an even keel all the time. People perceive this as "hardness," but it's just another wall I've put up to protect myself. I would be happier celebrating somebody else's big win than my own. I don't even secretly pat myself on the back; I always think I could have done it better. I'm never satisfied with myself. I want to keep growing and learning. Even when I win, I'm always thinking how I could do it better the next time.

I plan to ride as long as my body holds up and as long as I can stay successful. A lot of that has to do with fate; it's out of my control. If they decide to stop riding me, it doesn't matter how good I am. I've seen a lot of good riders who didn't get the opportunities to ride. There are a lot of components, including luck. As long as things are going my way, I'll be riding when I'm seventy-two if I can! It's not a money issue either. If I hit the lottery tomorrow, I'd still be doing this for the rest of my life. I just wouldn't have to put up much with the people I didn't choose to be with.

I'm not materialistic at all; my lifestyle is very simple. I love to save money. I don't enjoy spending on myself, but I love spending it on other people. I could live in a tent on a desert island as long as I had food and shelter; I don't need much. I do need outside stimulation from friends and family and affection from people and animals, especially dogs and horses. That's very important to me.

I used to be more of a rebel when I was younger; I felt a need to stand out. But now I like to blend in a bit and watch things happen. I see that as an evolution, not a stopping point, toward where I want to be. I've had a lot of very good influences in my life. My role model isn't a single person or something I've read; it's not a who or what. It would be my "higher self," to be very confident and happy within no matter what was happening around me, to be very much in control of my own emotions and not be influenced by others. It's just "a way of being" that is my role model. I'm working for that now; I'm changing things. Self-fulfillment and being happy within is what I need. I would like to give and receive equally. I find myself giving more than I will let myself receive. Most of all I long to be secure in every aspect of life; job, relationships, everything. I'm really very strong within and I know it, but I have a tendency to fall into weakness because it seems easier. But I never fall that far; something inside just clicks. I've found that everyone I have ever met has inspired me in a certain way. It's either, "Well, I definitely don't want to be that way," or "I definitely would like to feel that way." I've put those parts together for the ultimate person I want to be. I would like to be the person that someone else would like to be, to look up to.

To girls who want to be jockeys I would say above all, to go with their instincts. Go as far as they can in their education. I always thought school was a joke; I never took it seriously. I could have been an "A" student if I had applied myself. No one can ever learn enough, ever. Now I wish I could do it all again because even though I know I'm not, I feel very illiterate in a big world. I'm meeting all these people who know so much more than I do in all kinds of areas and I feel I know nothing by comparison. Girls should try to always do what they want and need to do to keep themselves happy. They should try to learn more than they think they will need. I've always been dyslexic; I could read, but I had a reading comprehension problem. Now that I'm thirty-one I'm going to get help with that because I feel I'm missing out on so much by not reading. I want to know so much. Besides education, girls should strive to be everything they want to be and more. They should do as much as they can, not get stuck in a rut. They must eat, do, say, see, feel something different everyday as often as they can. Ruts are too easy to get into and too hard to get out of. So if they're the best at one thing, they can be the best at two!

69

Darci Rice

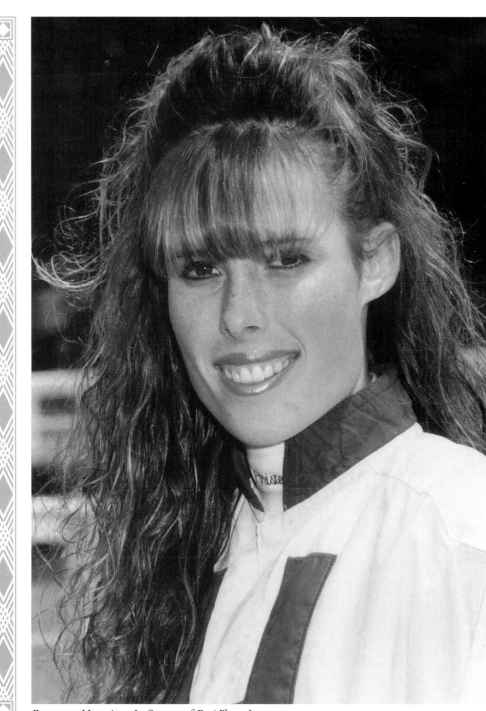

Rosemary Homeister, Jr. *Courtesy of Equi-Photo, Inc.*

Rosemary Homeister, Jr.

For Rosemary it all started with two sets of chromosomes imprinted with the word *horse*. She was nearly born and raised on the racetrack where her parents worked, rode, and trained horses for a living. Her mother is still one of the top Thoroughbred trainers in Florida, and although Rosemary rides for other barns, victory is never sweeter than when mother and daughter cross the finish line in first place as a team.

Many trips to the winner's circle and a professional, positive attitude throughout her career earned Rosemary the Eclipse Award, horseracing's equivalent to the Academy Award. She was the first women in racing history to receive it in 1995 for her work in 1992. She was also leading rider at the coveted Tropical Meet at Calder Racetrack in 1995. Monmouth Park honored her in New Jersey by having Rosemary Homeister, Jr., Day at their meet the following summer. In spite of all the respect the Thoroughbred industry has shown Rosemary, she states it is still an honor to be named on a horse when there are hundreds of riders out there to choose from.

It Was in the Genes

My mother started riding horses when she was seventeen in Lyndhurst, New Jersey. My grandfather used to take her out to a farm so she could learn how to ride because there was no way to have horses in her backyard—the houses were too close together. She went into show riding and had a horse of her own named Scarlet O'Hara. Wanting to learn more about horses and to find her independence, she decided to move to Florida. My Aunt Jan and Uncle Sam lived in Florida, so my grandfather drove her down. One morning they went over to the racetrack. The first barn they walked into belonged to Jimmy Croll. My mother started to hot walk horses for him in the mornings. My father-to-be happened to be galloping for Jimmy Croll at the same time; in fact he was galloping one great horse, Mr. Prospector. They started dating and married. I was born in Hollywood, Florida.

I was nearly born and raised on the racetrack. I've had ponies and horses my whole life because we lived on a farm in Rolling Oaks. We also had dogs, cats, chickens, and "a" cow. We were living in a trailer on the farm for a while because my father and grandfather were building our house. My father had one humongous rooster named Leroy, and Leroy just knew every morning what time I was going to wake up and walk out the door. I would open the trailer door and he would jump on the steps and attack me. He was so big that he would knock me down on the floor and land on top of me. My father would have to come and get him off me and put him back in his place. My father was the only person he would mind. I would yell, "Get that thing away from me."

We had chickens, though, that would lay huge, huge eggs. We were in the newspaper once because our chickens laid the biggest egg ever. I'll never forget that. After a few years, our house finally was finished, and it was wonderful.

My mother actually rode as a jockey before I was born. She rode for Larry Geiger on a winning horse named Winning News. She became pregnant shortly after that win, had me, and then started to train horses. She has been training horses ever since and loves it. She gets on all her horses, gets the feel of them, and then can tell riders exactly how the horses are jockey to jockey in addition to trainer to jockey because she's been there. She understands the pressures on jockeys. She doesn't give too many instructions, but she'll point out the horse's quirks, which is one of the most important things.

When I ride for her, we just click because I ride exactly the way she as a trainer wants me to ride. We are so close she doesn't have to say it, I just know what to do. She'll breeze the horses and let me know their quirks before a race. My mother and I are the best of friends; she is also like a sister and a mother all rolled into one. When I started riding for her, I was really nervous because I wanted to win so badly for her. I would knock myself, be really hard on myself if I didn't. But now I'm much more relaxed with it; we go to the paddock before the race, she says, "Good luck," and we have been so lucky. My mother has a 67 percent win percentage right now, and I've ridden all nine of her winners this year. It's been a lot of fun. My dad died when I was fourteen, but I feel he is still with me. There have been so many times I thought I was on my way down in a race, and someone just lifted my horse back up. When my horse did go down a couple of times, it was as if my father laid pillows down, and I fell onto "pillows on the track." I just know he's there with me; I can feel it.

Born and Raised on the Racetrack

My first inkling that I wanted to be a jockey was as soon as I could talk. I was always on the racetrack; I went to work with my mother. I slept in the car with the windows rolled down a little for air. When I was four or five years old, I went to work every morning at 4:00 A.M. My parents were divorced. My father came around 7:00 A.M. to bring me breakfast and help me get dressed. I walked around the racetrack; everyone knew me. I always liked to smile and be enthusiastic. I still like to make people feel at ease and to treat them as I would like to be treated. I like to make people happy. I'd rather give than receive because I love to see people smile. If I think I've hurt someone's feelings in any way, I'm crazy until I feel it's rectified. If people hurt my feelings, I try to say to myself, "Well, I don't think they really meant it." If I think they did mean it, I try to go and talk to them, ask them what happened. I can't stand to have anyone mad at me.

Needless to say, I've known all the people at Calder Racetrack a long, long time. I rode horses, show horses also, from the time I was little through junior high school. I was always with my mother at the racetrack. When I entered high school, I started cheerleading and hanging out with boys and friends. I didn't want to come to the track anymore. My mother had to trick me to come to the races; I wanted to go out with my friends.

After high school I attended one year of college. At the time I was breaking yearlings for my mother and Larry Lyons, whom she was dating. She wound up staying with Larry for ten years. Larry Lyons and two-year-old horses were, synonymous; he was the "two-year-old king" at the racetrack. I learned my sense of how to keep my hands really light because two year olds required that softness when teaching them to race. I couldn't lose my temper with them; I had to be very patient as if they were human babies. As I was teaching them, they were teaching me. It taught me to have patience. I worked for Larry and my mother breaking two year olds for two years.

It was time for me to get onto the racetrack. I was attending college classes and working with the yearlings at the same time. I thought I should be a computer programmer, but after working with the yearlings one day, I said, "Mom, I want to ride again." She said, "Fine, honey!" She didn't push me back into riding in my teen years; she let me be a teenager. She never said, "Oh, you're going to be a jockey." I decided I didn't want to go to school anymore.

When I came to the track, exercise people helped me work horses. The jockeys and the trainers gave me a lot of input. It was great. They were like my family; they all wanted to see me do well. It gave me a big boost and a lot of confidence. The first horse that I galloped on the track was memorable. I was between my mother and a girl named Kika, who also galloped for my mother. I thought I was going 100 mph on my horse. I thought, "Oh, my God, what am I doing?" Galloping on the farm was nice and slow. My mother said, "Relax, you're fine." I said, "Please, we have to slow down." My mother said, "We are going slow."

I wasn't used to riding with my legs up shorter in the stirrups. I really had to tone my leg muscles. But after that first work out, I said to my mother, "That was so awesome. I want to do it again!" I was hooked.

The first time I ever galloped on the racetrack I was on a two year old, and she dropped me right on the track. She spun around, and I fell off. My mother said, "Get up. Get up." She never let me cry or complain. When I subsequently took a tumble, she'd say, "You're fine, get up," before I had time to think if I was hurt. I used to get mad at her for that, but I'm so happy she did it. It was the best training I could have had. When horses come out of the gate, they sometimes stumble or clip heels, and if you fall, you don't want to stand there crying on the racetrack. When I have fallen off horses, I have been more concerned that they were all right than whether I was. My first reaction when I fall is "go to the horse." I'm an animal lover. I donate to all animal causes, including those for elephants, whales, and greyhounds. My dream is to have my own animal sanctuary when I finish my riding years. My cousin has been helping my aunt raise money for people who have mental illness, so when it comes time to have my sanctuary, I know I'll have some help.

The Fan Clubs

My mother and I were always very close and still are. We were "attached at the hip" when I was growing up. My grandparents are like my second parents. My mother was alone when my parents divorced; all she did was work, eat, and sleep. I spent all the summers away at my grand-

Rosemary Homeister, Jr.

Covered in mud but happy as I have just come from the winner's circle at Calder Racetrack and am being congratulated by my mom, horsetrainer Rosemary Homeister, Sr., and my grandfather, my biggest fan. *Courtesy of Scooter Davidson.*

parent's house, and to this day they are my biggest fans. My grandfather is my number one fan. All he does is talk about me. He wears my hat with my name on it. My mother and I bought him a winter jacket with my name on the back, and he wears it up north all the time. My grandfather goes to simulcasting every day that I'm riding, even if it is only in one race, and then calls me at night and explains to me how I rode the race with all the "horseracing lingo." It's so cute.

Growing up, I had a best friend named Dawn. We both had ponies, lived on farms, and went horseback riding all the time. When I entered high school, the other kids would say how lucky I was to have a horse and wanted to come over and ride. By that time, I wanted to go out, do my cheerleading. I was a teenager. My high school friends were fascinated that my mother trained horses and that we lived on a farm and that I rode, but I thought it was no big deal. It was a big deal to my friends, however. In those years we lived with Larry Lyons on his huge five-acre farm with a big barn and cats, dogs, horses, you name it. My friends came over and were in awe just brushing a horse. I figured they came over just to ride, but they were interested in the whole picture.

I find that I take extra time now and give extra love to the horses that I ride. I want them to feel comfortable; I'm constantly petting them and just loving them. I treat animals the way I want to be treated. A lot of people think animals are dumb, but they are not. When an animal does something, he's trying to tell me something. I look at horses the way I look at people: some are stuck-up, some are shy, some are friendly and out-going, and some are mean no matter how friendly and loving I am toward them. They have the same personalities as people, but they can't verbalize them, so they express them in other ways. They show their emotions with their ears, eyes, and gestures. I think I get along so well with animals because I see them as people; I pay attention to their vibes.

I was very fortunate growing up. My mother raised me right; I had to earn and work for everything. I'm really glad about that because I appreciate things a lot more. When people are handed things, they don't stop to realize how lucky they are to have them.

I believe in God and talk to God every day. I'm not a religious fanatic who goes to church all the time, but I'm very religious with myself. I try to do things in life that are right and that God would approve. For instance, if I stub my toe, I have to think, "What have I done wrong lately?" If I find myself complaining, I try to think of those less fortunate and wonder what I'm complaining about.

In addition to my wonderful family jockey Mary Russ was one of my role models. She has known me a long time. When I was young, I was so fascinated by the fact that she was a woman who was aggressive; she had a great personality. Whether she won or lost she kept the same poise and positive attitude. I think of her all the time still. I just sent her a Christmas card on which I had written, "You will always be my role model." When she started racing, it was so much tougher for a woman. People looked at racing as a man's sport. It's not a man's sport. They said that women weren't strong enough or able to handle the horses. Well, no one is "strong enough" to handle a fifteen hundred pound horse—period! If that horse wants to make a left-hand turn, it turns. No matter how strong a person is, she is like a rag doll on top! Horses mind because they are taught to obey, but if something startles them, well, they react. I used to get mad when a trainer said to me, "The owner doesn't think you're strong enough." I would say, "Well, who's strong enough then, I would like to know? Hercules, maybe?" I ride with a light hand and a long hold, and I like to sit and be patient.

Our Social Life Is Our Home Life

I socialize mostly with people in the horse industry. Jockey José Ferrer and I have been together since July 1993. We met at the racetrack and were riding together at the time. I was concentrating on my riding because I was an apprentice jockey and didn't get to know him that well. We had met in Florida but were both up north working. He was with an outfit that wanted to send some cheaper horses down to Atlantic City to race at night, and he didn't want to go, so I started going. I started to pick up a lot of his business. One particular trainer, Phil Serpe, (José was riding every horse in his barn) kept sending down horses that José didn't want to go down with, and I won and won and won on them. So I ended up getting into Phil Serpe's barn, and José basically got kicked out. We hadn't started to date yet.

I used to watch José ride because I liked his style; he's very aggressive but looks "pretty" on a horse. I used to try to learn by copying his style along with those of a few other riders. I took a little bit from each rider to develop my own style. José and I didn't talk much to each other then. He really didn't like me too much because I was taking his business. The next year I got hurt at the Meadowlands, was out for two months, and came back to Florida. The second year that I was riding, José and I became good friends. We ended up going out with each other and we have been together ever since. We just got engaged and bought a house together, so we hope we have a very long future together.

Rosemary Homeister, Jr.

75

With the love of my life, José C. Ferrer.
He is a jockey too, and besides that
we have so much in common.
Courtesy of Rosemary Homeister, Jr.
Photographer, Gloria Ferigno, deceased.

So what do two jockeys do in their off hours? Well, we're homebodies. We like to go home, watch TV, do things around the house. We don't go out dancing or to parties that much; we actually can't wait to get home at night. We like to decorate, clean and fix things. José and I are together almost twenty-four hours a day. We drive to work together, work all morning, ride all afternoon, go home. We have a really great, great relationship. We're best friends; we have such a bond; we really don't want to be with anybody else. We have friends but enjoy each other's company more. I tell him everything. I tell people, "If you tell me something and you don't want José to know, don't even tell me." He's like my diary; I tell him everything, then lock him up.

José and I almost never fight. In fact, I don't remember the last time we had an argument. If we disagree, we'll just talk to each other and ask, "Well, how come you disagree?" I'll tell my reason; he'll tell his. If we do snap at each other, it's because we have something else on our minds bothering us. It's not about each other. Then we comfort each other over it. We have very good communications together, and I love him to death!

My Advice

If I were talking to girls between the ages of ten and fourteen and they were telling me they wanted to be jockeys, I would tell them really to think about it—think about whether they could dedicate themselves to a jockey's life. A jockey's life, especially in the beginning when she has to establish herself, means waking up every day at 5:00 A.M. She can't weigh more than 105 pounds, and she must work seven days a week and on holidays. Racing goes on 365 days a year, and if she's not busy in one state, she has to go where she will be busy because in this business "out of sight is out of mind."

Being a jockey can be very stressful and fatiguing. When I am on a horse, I am working with my whole body and mind. The way I deal with stress now is different from the way I dealt with it when I first started. I'm good at it now; I've practiced. Girls should know it's not all glamour; it's not just jumping on a horse and jumping off. I have to do a lot of talking with people and have good communication skills. I have to dedicate my life to riding and thinking about racing, learning every day that I never stop learning. As in life, there is always something more to learn.

I would tell sixteen year olds that when I was their age, I didn't even want to be a jockey. I wanted to cheerlead and go out with boys. I had an attitude—"Don't tell me what to do," and "I'm going to do what I want when I want." Girls have to understand that being a jockey is not just a job, it's a career. They must be dedicated to that career to survive. They must be able to promote themselves, to talk and communicate, to show enthusiasm and to be good listeners. They must take in so much information, get a lot out of it, and not forget. One little mistake could be a big one in the future.

As a rider, I never know if a horse is going to go down and I'm going to get hurt. Every day after, every race I ride, after my horse pulls up past the finish line safely, I thank God. A horse could stumble, fall, or fall on top of me, so I always thank God and my dad because I know he's watching over me.

Even if I don't win a race, I always try to come back with something positive. People put a lot of love, time, and money into these horses, and they deserve respect from the riders. I'm never negative; I hate that. If something happens, it happens for a reason, and it's going to turn out to be positive. I always give encouragement and suggestions to the owners and trainers after I ride their horses. I feel it is an honor to be named on a horse when there are hundreds of riders out there from which to choose. I raced on a horse the other day and although we finished second, he ran so hard and tried so much to win that I got off him after the race and told him, "I'm so proud of you. You ran such a good race." And he looked at me as if to say, "Did we win?" I always compliment horses I finish last on because next time they'll be in a better spot. Good positive thoughts produce good positive results.

In racing I always say there are thrills, spills, and excitement. The possibility of injury is a real part of working with horses. A horse can stumble out of the gate; he can clip heels by riding too close to another horse; there are many split-second decisions. I had only one very bad spill at the Meadowlands on a horse named Toymaker. My horse was five lengths ahead on the lead and we were going 35 mph. I switched the stick to my other hand, and the horse jumped the inner turf rail and didn't make it. The rail came down and punctured my hip and broke my iliac crest. The horse's neck was punctured also, but she survived and is still running today. I was out of racing for

77

Rosemary Homeister, Jr.

two months, but I choose to remember all my safe rides and the great horses and people with whom I've worked.

I Was Just Being Myself

I have no rivalries with other girl jockeys now, but when I was first riding up north as an apprentice, a lot of girls were riding, and there were jealousies. Down in Florida just Katie Sweeney and I were riding when I first started. Katie did very well as an apprentice but not so well after she lost her "bug." She was jealous when I started to do well, which showed in her attitude toward me. I was very timid in the beginning and, of course, didn't like it when anyone was mad at me. She was so mean to me. I tried to ignore her and stay out of her way. One day she came up to me and started crying and apologizing, saying, "I'm sorry I've treated you like this. You haven't done anything. I'm really happy for you. I'm just unhappy that I'm not doing as well." Then I started crying. It made me feel better, and at the same time it made her feel better because she knew that I hadn't done anything to her.

So I had a little taste of it. Then when I went up north, forget it, those girls were so mean to me. When I rode in Atlantic City, there were fifteen girls in one little jockey's room. I came to Atlantic City Racecourse with Monmouth Park shippers; these horses were like rockets. If I didn't fall off the horse out of the gate, I won; that's how good these horses were. When I walked in that jockey's room, they all turned their heads away and wouldn't look at me. As soon as I walked by they turned their heads back around. If one of the other girls won a race, when she came back into the room, they would all yell, "Congratulations." If I won a race, I'd walk back in to silence. I would just get dressed and leave. This went on for about two months, and I cried to my agent, "I don't want to go there anymore." It hurt my feelings. I never tried to rub the wins in their faces; I was just being myself. I was just doing my job, winning for the trainers who hired me to ride their horses. I had to learn to deal with it, and it was difficult for me because I'm a very sensitive person. But it only went on for the first six months of my career, and now, if it ever happened again, I could handle it.

Then I met Julie Krone. When I met her in the jockey's room, I would just look at her and think, "I can't believe I'm sitting in the same room as Julie Krone." She would be just talking away like her happy self, and I would be thinking to myself, "Oh my God, I'm really sitting with Julie Krone." I'll never forget that. She was like a celebrity to me and still is. There is nobody like her. She can make me feel so wonderful. I can be as low as the ground and she can uplift me to the sky. She knows exactly the right words to say to make me feel great. When I was learning to ride, my mother would make me watch all the reruns of the races at night on the television. Gulfstream was the "on" track and my mother would say, "Watch Julie Krone, she's the best," and my mother wanted me to be the best. Just yesterday Julie was telling me, "You're so beautiful; you're so great; you're riding so well." I had to say, "Julie, you're making me feel so good, I'm going to burst!" I think she is so neat, and I wish her success forever. There will never be anyone like her. She laid big stepping stones down for all of us. Others opened the door for us, but Julie blew it wide open.

Jockey Paula Bruno is also one of my best friends. When I met her, she was just learning to ride. I clicked with her immediately. I don't have a lot of girls as friends because they are either envious or I don't know what. I try to help them with riding, and they look at me as if to say, "I don't want your help." I love to see everyone do well whether it's a boy or a girl, and I like to help if I can. I've learned though when I first encounter people, especially women, not to say too much because I don't want them to think I'm telling them what to do. With Paula, it was an instant liking on both our parts. She has such a great attitude and is so good at so many things. She has so many professions in addition to being a jockey. She's a nurse, a chiropractor, a farm manager, a riding instructor, she can do anything. She used to give me massages when we worked at the Meadowlands. She would bring her massage table and massage me twice a week. So she was my massage therapist, my best friend, and a great person to talk to. I helped her with her riding. She would come in after a race and ask what I thought. I would give her some suggestions: do it this way, try this, and so forth, and she would say, "Okay." Most people wouldn't be that open. We would go over the racing form together. It took me a while to figure out all the information in the form, especially because they keep adding things. I write my own little symbols in the form. I explained to Paula that when we look at the racing form, it's to see where we'll probably be in the race with our horses, not who is going to win; that's for the bettors. Paula and I would go over the form together, which also helped me a lot. She won a Grade III race the other day for Allen Jerkens; I'm so proud of her. I really like Mr. Jerkens. I don't know him that well, but I know he helps a lot of people. He wants everyone to do well, like I do. He will give a rider whom he thinks is starving a shot to prove himself. He's a really great man.

Accomplishments and Acknowledgments

I was given the Eclipse Award three years later because Jesus Bracho, the apprentice jockey who did get the award that year, falsified his records. He forfeited the Eclipse Award and his lead-

79

The first and only women ever to receive the Eclipse Award in 1995 for my work in 1992.
Courtesy of Rosemary Homeister, Jr.

Rosemary Homeister, Jr.

ing rider title at Calder. So I wound up getting the Eclipse Award and the leading rider award for the Tropical Meet at Calder for 1992. I'm the first and only woman ever to receive the Eclipse Award. When I found out, I was in the Meadowlands jockey room. They sent a fax down with the news. I was so happy and all the other jockeys and the clerk of scales were happy for me; I was bouncing all over the room.

I attended the 1995 Eclipse Award dinner, and we sat with Dale Beckner, who received the award that year, and his family. I was so nervous when they finally called my name to come up to the front, that I left the little speech I had prepared back at the table. So I didn't get to say all the things I had written down, but I did say the most important thing—I thanked my mother for helping me and for being there through everything, and I thanked my father because I felt him with me all the time. I wanted to thank the trainers and the grooms and everyone, but I was shaking like a leaf. When I got the award in my hand, I wanted to kiss it. I kept staring at it all through dinner. My fiancé and my mother, the two most important people in my life, were with me, so it was a great night.

The award is in the kitchen of our new house. All our awards and trophies are up on top of the cabinets where we can see them every day. We spend a lot of time in the kitchen. I got a lot of publicity from the Eclipse Award. Monmouth Park had a "Rosemary Homeister Day" in 1995 on the second day of the meet. They printed two thousand pictures of me and had my name up on the billboards. It was so thrilling. People were so interested in meeting me, and I couldn't believe how many people kept up with my career. They would say, "I remember you when you first rode at so and so." The racing fans still put me up on a pedestal and make me feel so wonderful. But I feel *they* are so wonderful, and it's because of them that I am here. The fame I have is from their support. They are like a big family pushing for me, "Go Rosemary, go."

I thank all my fans for their support and fan mail and birthday cards. I try to write everyone back and to send thank-you cards. A man from California actually knew my father when he rode. He wrote me two letters with stories about my father, and I just cried, it was so neat. I never know whom I'll meet. He found me by seeing an article on me in *Bloodlines* magazine. When he saw the name Homeister, he wondered if I could be his friend's daughter, and I was.

I really thank all the owners who have had the confidence to put me on all their horses. I know they put so much money into these horses, and they don't get to spend a lot of time with them. They are mostly in the background, and when their horses are out racing, they have to be confident that the riders are going to take care of them, making sure the horses don't get hurt and at the same time trying to win. It brings such joy to everyone to be in the winner's circle.

I'm thankful to the trainers. They are out there every day with the horses, who are like their kids. It's a lot of stress sometimes for them. They have to make sure the horses are okay, that they slept okay, that they're eating all right, that they don't have fevers in the morning.

The grooms are a very, very important part of racing and horses. They probably spend the most time with the horses. The horses are their meal tickets. When their horses do well and win, I always reward the grooms. They really are just as important to winning as everybody else. They love the horses so much. They do everything to take care of the horses—clean the stalls, feed them, brush them—and are sensitive to their changes. If something happens to their horse, it's like it's happening to one of their kids. Their work comes from the bottom of their hearts. The groom is the most important part of owning a Thoroughbred. A trainer has to have a groom he can trust who loves the horse. Grooms don't get the appreciation that they should. Each groom has three to four horses under his care, which is quite a handful. Grooms usually are up at 4:00 A.M. and have to be around all day to satisfy their horse's needs. The racetrack usually provides living quarters right on the backstretch for them because they don't earn a lot of money and have to be on call if trainers needs something for their horses. Sometimes I feel so bad because they work so hard and get so little money. During the afternoon pony people ride out onto the track with the horses before the race. They help to keep the horses calm. They are like the horses' buddies and are important to the horses and to us riders as well. Sometimes my horse will want to follow the pony instead of going into the gate, as if to say, "Wait, I'd rather go with you!"

Even though the trainers have a lot to do, the assistant trainers do most of the hard work. A lot of assistant trainers are there with the horses twenty-four hours a day, like the grooms. They have to make sure things are right and oversee the grooms. They don't get their names in the programs and they don't get the recognition that the trainers get, but they work harder than anyone in the barn.

All the horses are special to me, and I love them all but certain ones stand out for me. One horse in particular died last year, and broke my heart, and I still think of him all the time. I felt he was like my own horse; I saw him everyday and he had such a personality. He used to scratch my back with his teeth, and I would scratch him. I was riding him last year in a race, and he dropped dead. I was trying to ease his pain, but the vet said he died before he felt any pain. I couldn't believe I was riding him when it happened. It took me a while to get over it. I miss him so much. He was a part of me. His name was Better Love Me. I'll never, ever forget him.

Then there is Don Cyan. He is awesome and so grand with a beautiful body and a big, big head with a white blaze. I won four races on him for my mother; she trained him. I loved Don Cyan so much that I purchased him when he retired from racing. His owners were wonderful people. I won eight races on Stalwart Pleasure, and she is still running up at Penn National. Bon Bon D'or is my best horse this year. Danny Hurtack trains him. I won eight races on him just this summer, and he's still going. He first ran at $12,500, and now he's at $45,000. He's an incredible horse; they don't know where to run him next. Dancing Jason and American Honor are both trained by Emanuel Berrios, and I won seven races on each one of them. Flying Concert was one of my best horses this year also. I won two stakes races on her.

Riding for my mother is easy now although I used to be nervous because I wanted to win for her so bad. I wanted not to make any mistakes and for the race to set up perfectly. When I win for her, it feels like my biggest accomplishment. She doesn't want to ride anyone else but me because

Rosemary Homeister, Jr.

Winning for my mother
(Rosemary Homeister, Sr., third
from left) on horses she trains—my
biggest accomplishment.
Courtesy of Jean Raftery.

A.Vitti's
Air Mike,2nd
Mollys Pot Shot,3rd
6 Furlongs
1:10 4/5

Buttonwood

Don Cyan

Calder Race Course

Rosemary Homeister,Jr.,up
Rosemary Homeister,Trainer
June 21,1996
Copyright
Jean Raftery

she knows I'm going to give her not only every effort and the best ride but also that I'll ride the way she would. It's as if she were on the horse. If we don't win, I'll come back and we'll discuss it and try something different the next time out. Some horses can race again in a week; some need three to four weeks. Horses use so much energy and adrenaline when they run, they can lose up to one hundred pounds during a race and need to replenish their electrolytes. The trainer needs to build them back up again and get their confidence back. So much goes into training; it's like training a professional human athlete. My mother usually has between five and eight horses in her barn.

My mom always asks me, "When you're done riding, do you think you'll want to train?" She would love to see me become a trainer. First she wanted me to be a jockey; now she wants me to be a trainer. I really haven't thought about it because I want to ride forever. I don't know if I would be a good trainer because I would fall in love with each of the horses, and then if they were claimed, I would be heartbroken—"There goes my baby." Or if they got sick, I would be so worried. So that decision is a long way off yet.

I love to do other sports. I love to jet-ski. I love doing crafts. I make covered photo albums. I love computers and make my own stationary and labels. I love to do laundry and fold laundry. My fiancé will tell you it's one of the things he loves best about me. I love to watch football. Every Sunday I'm glued to the TV. People outside racing say to me, "Oh, you have no life. You have to get up so early and you never go out." But I have a wonderful life; I socialize all day long! I do what I enjoy. I get up in the morning, and I say, "Oh good, I get to go to work." How many people can say that?

I love spending time with José, my fiancé. We have so much in common, and he is so wonderful. He helps me deal with work pressure. I'm very hard on myself. I always want to look good and feel good. He's always there telling me I'm beautiful and keeping my confidence up. I can always tell when something is bothering him, and I know how to get him to talk about it and comfort him. I love to see him smile. We are so compatible, and my family really loves him. When he proposed to me on Christmas Day, it was the best. We were both nervous; he was shaking and I was shaking. I don't know how he got the ring on my finger. He recited a speech in front of my whole family and told them how much he loves me and how he wants to marry me and be with me for the rest of his life. I started crying; then everyone started crying. I can't explain all the feelings but it was one of the best days of my life.

Rosemary Homeister, Jr.

Donna Barton. *Courtesy of Frank Anderson.*

Donna Barton

"Like mother, like daughter" is a wonderful compliment in the Barton family. Donna, daughter of famed pioneer female jockey Patti Barton-Brown, wanted to be anything but a jockey growing up. But slowly, after four years of galloping horses for trainers such as Jack Van Berg, she decided at twenty-one years of age it was time to get serious about a career. And get serious she did, putting mind and body skills together and sky-rocketing to the top, riding winners home for D. Wayne Lukas among other notable trainers. Of the first eleven horses Mr. Lukas put her on at their first meet at Turfway Park, she won with ten, then brought the eleventh one to the winner's circle at Keenland Racetrack one month later. She is one of the few women ever to ride in the Breeder's Cup. She brought a horse named Hennesey to a second place finish in that race in 1995, and the horse's owner praised her on national television for her ride. In 1996 she broke the record at Churchill Downs, home of the Kentucky Derby, for the most races ever won by a female rider and then broke her own record by two one year later.

Like Mother Like Daughter

I was born in Alamogordo, New Mexico, in 1966. My sister, who is 2 years and 8 months older than I am, was born in Los Angeles. My brother, who is 360 days younger than I am, also was born in Alamogordo. My mother, Patti Barton, started riding as a jockey when I was two. Her first husband was our father, Charlie Barton. She divorced him when my brother was six months old. We stayed with my grandmother and other people for about three to four years when we were young because my father was financially unable to support us and my mother knew it was going to be a long time before she could support us properly.

My mother wanted to start riding. She was one of the first half-dozen women to be licensed as jockeys in the United States, and she knew she had a journey ahead of her just to do that, much less try to support three children as well. She won her first race on May 30, 1969 at Pikes Peak in Colorado. She ended up settling in West Virginia and riding at Waterford Park in 1969. The first year she rode she won 179 races. Of course, at the time it was a record. No woman had ever won that many races. For nineteen years, from the time she started riding in 1969, she held the world's record for the most wins by a female. She retired in 1984 after a very bad spill with 1,202 wins to her credit, "recorded victories," as she likes to say, because that didn't include wins on quarter horses or wins out of the country. It was 1988 before Julie Krone and Patti Cooksey in the same week surpassed my mother's record. So you can imagine the jump she had on all the women who were riding.

We moved back in with my mother when I was six. A lot of my childhood around those years is cloudy to me. We moved to West Virginia and lived there until I was nine. Then we moved to Pennsylvania. Then we moved to Kentucky. My mother remarried, and we moved near Fairmont Park.

My mother had always loved horses. She was adopted as a baby, and the family who adopted her didn't tell her she was adopted until she was seventeen. It was evident her whole life that she wasn't from the same lineage because they all wanted her to be a telephone operator. If she could just have been a telephone operator, they would have been so proud of her. She hated dresses; she didn't want to be a telephone operator.

When she was fourteen, I believe, she started mowing lawns and cleaning stalls to save up enough money to buy a horse. By the time she was fifteen she had bought her first horse. She had to go to the stables and work around the barn to pay for her horse's board, and she mowed more lawns for his feed. Her mother hated it so badly that even at the age of fifteen when my mother came home from the stables she had to take off all her clothes on the porch. She had to strip to her underpants before she could come in the house. Her mother really thought she was making the wrong choice; at the time she just didn't think it was a good occupation for a girl.

My mom went against everyone to pursue her love for horses. When she met my father she was a trick rider in the rodeo. She broke and rode bulls. Before she had my sister, she was a card

A taste in 1973 of what it was like to win my first blue ribbon.
Courtesy of the Barton family.

dealer in Las Vegas and a truck driver; the stuff she did back then was incredible. My father at the time they met was a cowboy in the rodeo; he broke bulls and all that. She just fell in love with him. He was sixteen years older than she was. He was a beer-drinking cowboy, and she didn't realize until she married him that he was an alcoholic. He never planned on being anything but a cowboy, and now she had three small children. She tended bar and began to gallop horses on the racetrack during those years. Her initial reason for wanting to become a licensed jockey was for the workman's compensation. If she got hurt as an exercise rider, she would get twelve dollars a week, but if she were a licensed jockey, she would get fifty dollars a week. She knew she could feed us on fifty dollars a week, but not on twelve.

Everyone I Knew and Was Related to Was a Jockey

I grew up never ever wanting to be a jockey. When I left high school, I went to the racetrack to try to earn enough money to pay my way through college. I wasn't galloping or exercising horses yet, just grooming. It didn't take long to realize that I couldn't earn enough money doing that, and it took too much time. So I thought, I'll start galloping horses and then I'll be able to pay my way through college. To start to gallop horses in the morning I had to practice and learn to apply my trade before it became marketable. In the beginning people basically prefer riders to pay them to get on their horses because they're not good riders yet. By the time I was making pretty decent money galloping horses (and by decent money I mean $250 a week), I liked what I was doing. I knew my career probably would have something to do with horses although I didn't know what then.

My brother started riding as a jockey when he was sixteen, my sister at nineteen although she galloped and rode quarter horses from the time she was seventeen. They both wanted to be jockeys when they were growing up; I wanted to be anything but a jockey. Everyone I knew was a jockey; everyone I was related to was a jockey; and all their friends were jockeys. I, well, I was a rebel. I did well in school; I liked school. One thing I could do was argue, so I thought I could be a good lawyer. I never had any interest in politics. Because of my love for animals the thought of becoming a veterinarian crossed my mind a couple of times until I saw big gaping wounds. I threw out that idea.

At any rate, I was galloping horses on the racetrack. I worked for Jack Van Berg for two and one-half years. That was nice, and I felt like I was part of the outfit. Van Berg is famous for being a slave driver, and I had to work hard, but he made me feel a part of it. In the end I galloped horses for four and one-half years.

I was in Birmingham, Alabama, when an owner from Kentucky got hold of me about training some horses. He had been a friend of my family's for a long time, and had some cheap horses, about ten of them. He wanted to change trainers. I was twenty-one at the time, and I thought it was about time I became serious about something. He knew I had been galloping horses for a long time. And it was time, even if I didn't think so.

Donna Barton

There was an agent at the racetrack in Birmingham at the time named Pete Antonucci. He had been trying to talk me into riding races for two years saying, "If you ever want to ride, I'd like to hustle your book." So I went to Pete and told him about this offer from Kentucky. A big thing with me at the time was that I had grown up listening to all these stories about where everybody was, where everyone traveled to. So when I was galloping horses, I didn't want to stay in one place. I wanted to go to all those tracks. I wanted to be the one able to sit around and tell where everybody was, where I went and what I did, different racetracks, different states. When I was galloping for those four and one-half years I did travel quite a bit, even when I worked for Van Berg. In fact, I worked for him from Detroit to Louisiana to Kentucky.

When I had done enough traveling, I mentioned it to Pete. He said, "Well, if you want to try riding, I can have you on a horse next week." I said, "Okay, I want to try riding a race." At the time I had long hair past my shoulders, and I smoked cigarettes. I had smoked for eight years. I thought nobody would take me seriously unless I looked like a jockey. All the jockeys had short hair and didn't wear makeup; well, the guys didn't wear makeup. I wanted to look like a guy jockey. I quit smoking cigarettes. I knew if I wanted to be an athlete I couldn't be a smoker. I got rid of that permanent habit quickly because I had such a good reason. I was going to try riding, that's all. I thought if riding and being an athlete was not for me, I could go back to smoking. It's now ten years later, and I still don't smoke.

So I quit smoking and cut off all my hair. The next day when I went to the track everyone called me "Don" Barton. As it happened, I had told the hairdresser just to cut off the back of my hair and to leave my bangs. Well, snip, snip, he cut my bangs off as well as my hair in the back. I said, "You cut off all my bangs!" He said, "Oh yeah, I did, didn't I. Well, I'll take a few dollars off the price of your haircut," so instead of an eleven dollar haircut I had a five dollar one, and I looked like a boy. It was such a drastic change, but at least everybody took me seriously.

Challenge and Excitement

Two weeks after I talked to Pete, he got me on a horse. I rode the race. It was uneventful. I came in fifth, midpack. My brother came to see me. He had already quit riding by then and was passing through Birmingham on his way to California. He took pictures of me in the paddock. When I came back from the race and pulled up to the unsaddling area, I saw him, so I just jumped off the horse and said, "Wow, that was really cool." He said, "Donna, go unsaddle your horse." I looked back, and the trainer was unsaddling him, just looking at me like, "What?" But it was so exciting, and I hadn't expected it to be. I got the taste for it.

When I was a gallop person in the mornings, I wanted to train rather than ride because it seemed so much more challenging mentally. I guess I thought that way because I grew up around riding. I didn't realize how challenging riding was until I rode my first race. There were so many things even after my first race that I wanted to try and do differently. On May 30, 1997, I had been riding for ten years but there was still always something new to practice on the equisizer in my garage. Riders make it look easy, and there is nothing easy about it. I didn't realize that at first. That is probably what challenged me to do it, and it's also part of what made me want to quit about five times, especially in the early stages. I thought, "I'm just not going to get it," or "It's just too hard"—the same career struggles people in other professions go through. In a line in the movie *A League of Their Own* Geena Davis's character says, "But it's so hard," and Tom Hank's character says, "If it were easy, everyone would do it," and that's the truth.

After I started riding, it didn't take me long to win my first race. I had some early support from two trainers; their horses comprised the majority of my first ten wins. I wound up winning my first fifteen races in Birmingham. I went on to Rockingham Park to finish my apprenticeship and shared the same agent with Diane Nelson for awhile. Diane was recovering from a back injury, and her agent heard that I had some promise. He happened to be passing through Birmingham and on the day he was there I got so lucky I had my eleventh, twelfth, and thirteenth wins on the same day. It was fate. He told me going in, "I'm not here to watch you ride. I'm going to take your book anyway." It was meant to be.

I went to Rockingham Park for about eight months; with two months remaining in my apprenticeship, I didn't want to lose my "bug" up there. I got hold of Pete Antonucci again. He was at Canterbury Downs and had enough pull with leading trainer Greg Markraf to get me mounts that I could keep. I went; the meet had just started, and I won three out of my first five races there. I thought, "God, thank you, thank you, thank you." To be honest, I would never be able to endure any long periods of losing. I'm not a good loser. I was complaining to Julie Krone once when I was going through a bad spell, and she said, "Donna, a good loser is still a loser. Don't ever get used to being a loser." Just because I don't like to lose, doesn't mean I never lose. It just seems whenever I've needed things to click right, they always have.

Spiritually, from the time I was nine years old I have known there is a God. In a little incident God showed himself to me, and I've always prayed a lot about different things. Even when I'm in a period of not praying, it seems that God is always guiding my life.

After I had won my first four races in Birmingham I was going to the gate, and I have to say I was still trying to make up my mind, "Am I going to do this or not?" I was on a horse that was a complete rat! She was so bad, washed out from head to toe, and she kept trying to throw herself down and flip over. I took my feet out of the irons and basically took myself out of the situation and started praying. I said, "God, this is obviously not what you had in mind for me. It has gotten to where it is way too difficult and the horses are just too bad and I'm having to work too hard for so little reward. So that's it, I quit. Thanks for showing it to me, and thanks for letting me realize it's not for me." And of course, the horse won. She won by a nose. I beat a horse ridden by Julio Espinoza, who at the time was coming off his sixteenth leading rider title at Churchill Downs. So I said, "Okay, God, this is for me. I get the message." There have been so many times that I have asked God and actually listened to Him that He has guided me in one direction or another. Inevitably, whenever something is right,

Donna Barton

He shows it to me just like that—like the day that Curt, my agent, came to Birmingham. I won three races in one day. When I went to Canterbury Downs, I won my first three races, then a second, then two more wins. When I first came to Keenland in the fall of 1993, arriving the night before I had to ride four mounts; I won on three of them. It was opening day of the meets and I was leading rider.

I Thought You Might Like to Know...

From Birmingham I went to Rockingham in the fall of 1987 and in 1988 to Canterbury Downs. In the winter of 1988 I went to Oklahoma for their inaugural season into 1989, then back to Canterbury Downs for the summer of 1990, back to Oklahoma for 1990–91, then back to Canterbury for the summer of 1991, back to Oklahoma in the winter of 1992, then to Chicago in the summer of 1993. That was when I decided to go to Florida for the winter of 1993–94, stopping at Keenland and Churchhill Downs to ride the 1993 fall meets.

Since I began riding 1987, I had always wanted to go to Kentucky because my sister was there and because I remembered my mother saying that of the 1,202 races she won, the race she rode at Keenland stood out in her mind because of the prestige of the meet. But I always thought it would be too tough. So in 1993, on the second day of the Keenland meet, I went over to D. Wayne Lukas's barn. I said, "Hi, you don't know me, but I'm Donna Barton, and I won three races here yesterday, which makes me leading rider. I know you always want to ride the hot hand, and I thought you might like to know who I am. I just came over here to tell you that." He laughed. He thought I was a cocky little thing, I guess. He told me later that as I walked away he had no intention of ever riding me that day.

I went to Gulfstream Park in Florida for the winter of 1993–94 and 1994–95, and they were the worst two winters of my life. A lot of riders go down to Gulfstream expecting to only ride a little, and I was all right with that for the first two weeks. Then I wanted to ride more horses. I was riding two a day, and I wanted to ride five. So I had to go out and work a little harder, get there a little earlier, and see more people. And guess what, it didn't matter! They didn't need me to work horses; they had their gallop people. Jerry Bailey and Mike Smith were still going to get the best horses, and I just couldn't take it. I felt the purses were awful for the level of competition I would be dealing with there. The purses were better, or at least as good, at Turfway Park in Kentucky, and I could ride five to seven a day. Granted, it's cold, but I leave the jock's room, go to the paddock, run to the gate on my horse, ride the race, pull up, and run back into the jock's room. I have my thermals on. I can handle it; I'm riding races, making money, and as far as I'm concerned, that's what makes me happy.

I started riding horses before I can even remember. I remember my first spill when I was about five years old. A horse threw me into a fence. I have scars all over my face from that, but they are small. In fact, if I wanted to remember them all, I'd have to get out a magnifying glass.

What I learned from moving around so much when we were little is that it's okay to be in different schools up until high school. I learned to adapt and to meet new people easily when I was younger. If I had the choice and had kids, I wouldn't necessarily want them to grow up moving as much as I did. If they want a good education or want to pursue an athletic endeavor, they really need to be in high school in one place.

My Mother, My Strength, My Role Model

My mother was a pillar of strength to me. I didn't live with my mother or father from when I was two until I was six; my brother and sister didn't either. We all lived with other people during those years. My mother displayed a huge amount of love before and after and also somewhat during the separation so all of us could come away from that not emotionally scarred or thinking our parents didn't love us. Never in my whole life did I ever think my mother didn't love me. I felt she loved me so much that she gave me up for awhile so I could have a good life. The whole time I was growing up I could go to my mother with anything and still can. The other day I was having a personal conversation on the telephone, and I said something to my mom, who was sitting beside me. The person on the line said, "You would talk like that in front of your mother?" I said, "I would say anything in front of my mother. There isn't a thing she doesn't know about me. I wouldn't keep anything from my mother."

In 1984 my mom had her really bad spill, and I was devastated. My brother and sister were devastated . The mother we had grown up with was "gone." She had brain damage and was in intensive care for two weeks. I can scarcely talk about it without crying. When she got out of intensive care, she wasn't the "same" lady I had grown up with. I went to a friend of mine and said, "How am I ever going to be happy again? My mother is never going to be the same. I can't understand how I'm supposed to go on and just live my life as if nothing has happened? It's not fair! She worked all those years, raising three kids and attending college for nine years, all at the same time so that if anything ever happened to her she would still be able to support us. And now she has brain damage and can't remember any of that and can't get a job." My friend said, "You just have to pray about it."

I was going from Louisiana Downs to the Fairgrounds for the winter, and it was a six-hour drive. I prayed probably the whole time, and when I got there, I realized a few things had happened. One, my mom was thirty-nine years old when the spill happened and she had planned to retire when she was forty, or so she says. She wouldn't have retired because she didn't have the financial means to retire. Two, it weaned me because I couldn't have taken my mother dying right then. If something had happened and she had just died, I would have lost it. I was nineteen at the time. You would have thought I would have been weaned by then, living away from home for two years, but I called her all the time about anything. She was so smart and thought things out so well that when she gave me advice, I would think, "Why didn't I think of that?" My mother was always an innovative thinker. She was before her time in a lot of areas.

During her recovery my mother settled a lawsuit, which wasn't a huge amount of money but she'll always be provided for. She had ridden mostly at cheaper tracks, and she hadn't earned a lot of money. Any money she did earn during all those years she spent on us kids.

Donna Barton

My mother was my strength and my role model in my life. When I was younger and I didn't want to be a jockey, it didn't mean that I didn't want to be like her; I did. My sister was also my strength. She was older and my mom was busy, so I would go to her if I needed something and she would take care of me. She would never feel sorry for me, though, like I wanted her to, so I felt we didn't get along from the time I was twelve to about seventeen. I wanted to be the baby, and no one ever let me. And now I'm so glad that nobody ever let me! I don't have to go to therapy, I'm not blaming anyone for anything that ever happened to me, and I assume full responsibility for myself. A lot of that self-reliance is the result of my sister helping me, but it didn't seem like help at the time.

A lot of people ask me, "Do you know it's tougher for you because you're a girl?" I don't mean to answer like a smart-aleck, but I say, "How would I know? I've never been a guy." Yeah, it's tough, but I see it being tough for a lot of people. Maybe it's to my advantage. If I go to a new track and there are ten new riders, nine guys and me, maybe I'll stand out from them. I was never raised with any of that gender stuff.

One of the great things about having a mom like I did was that I never remember her telling me that I couldn't or I shouldn't or because I'm a girl I couldn't do this or that. She never told my brother he couldn't cry because he was a boy. She never told me I had to wear dresses because I was a girl, and we agreed early on about that.

I still hear a lot of the other girl riders saying it's tougher for them because they're girls, and I think, "Well, how do you know that?" Maybe it's something their dads told them. I also hear excuses from a lot of girl riders who just aren't that good. They can blame it on whatever they want if they have to, but they have to work on themselves to improve.

There are negative cycles in every career. All of the biggest name jockeys have gone through it. Everyone just has to keep on keeping on. Keep going. People would ask my mother, "Do you want your kids to be jockeys?" She would say, "I neither encourage or discourage them; they can be whatever they want to be as long as they're good at it!" My sister became a jockey; her husband was a jockey; and she got married when she was nineteen. She quit riding when she got pregnant with her first child and stayed out for two years. She went back to riding about the same time I started to ride. She got pregnant with her second child and stopped riding. She never intended her career to be illustrious; she did it because she enjoyed the competition and the horses. She has four children now. My brother started riding when he was sixteen, but he couldn't get in with the lightweights, and by the time he was eighteen he knew he was going to be too big to have a career as a jockey. Now he's 5'10.5", 160 lbs., and very lean, but it's obvious why he had to quit. He was such a good rider, though, probably the best in the family. He is one of D. Wayne Lukas's assistants now and has three kids.

I've been lucky that my career hasn't been plagued with injuries. If it had been I don't know if I would be in the same place. In the ten years that I've been riding I've broken my nose four times, had six concussions, cracked a vertebrae in my neck, broken my collarbone, and broken my rib.

That's basically an injury-free career for a rider. Most of these injuries aren't a "time off" in my sport. I try to be cautious, of course, but I don't go into a race with a fear of injury. When I broke my collarbone and rib at the same time, I was working a horse in the morning. She did some very irrational things before the morning of the incident; for example, she'd be galloping along and suddenly turn around and go the other way. That's what she did that morning, I fell off, landed on my shoulder, and broke my collarbone. Did I ever want to ride her again? No. But that was just that horse. I didn't ever think another horse would do that to me because no horse ever did. I've also in my career taken on riding some horses that other people wouldn't ride.

When I first started riding, I hated the way I rode. I watched myself on video replay, and it was not what I had in mind. I was on the racetrack my whole life. I knew what a good rider looked like and rode like. I was not a good rider. I didn't even think I was getting away with it. But I couldn't make my body do what my mind wanted it to do. That is why I had to watch Julie Krone.

Julie was a girl doing it, so I had to be able to do it. It was training certain muscles that hadn't been trained until that point. Now, I look just like the other riders, and I know it came from watching Julie. I had seen other girl riders but they couldn't ride like Julie Krone could. Julie is one of my very best friends.

I have some friends outside the horse industry and am consciously seeking more now. I want to be able to get some feedback from people outside the industry on how they feel about horse racing. But because of our schedules, most of my close friends are on the racetrack. Our weekend there is Monday and Tuesday.

The 1990s have become an age of information. It's a time where people are constantly trying to improve themselves and work harder and harder. I now am more tolerant than I was before of what we do compared to other people. Jockeys work so hard, love the horses, and put in long hours, but people relate to that because they are doing the same in their careers and lives. If I don't stay ahead or on top of things, I will fall way behind.

When I came back to Kentucky after a depressing winter at Gulfstream Park, my confidence was low. Even though I had won six races there during the meet, I knew I needed some good horses to ride to lift me out of my slump. So in the spring of 1994 I started to go by D. Wayne Lukas's barn again every morning at 5:00 A.M. because the other agents and jockeys would start showing up at 5:30 A.M. Wayne got there at 4:30 A.M., so it gave him enough time to get settled if I stopped to visit with him at 5:00 A.M., and I didn't cut into anyone else's time. The great thing about Wayne and me was that we instantly could get on the same "page" in any conversation we struck up. I don't know whether it was fate or destiny or what, but no one can make something like that happen. We just happened to click. We also had the same opinion on things, especially about racing. We saw things the same.

I rode for Steve Asmussen, and Wayne knew Keith Asmussen, Steve's father, very well. He must have put some credibility in the fact that if they rode me, I must have been doing something right. He trusted their horsemanship. So Wayne started to let me work some horses in the morning. That went really well. He was happy with the way I sat on his horses and followed his instructions. He was glad I had a good clock in my head.

Wayne started to let me ride some of his first-time starters, the two year olds. Pat Day and those guys don't need to ride the two-year-old first-timer starters. They will for Wayne, but they usually don't want to. It went well for us. Wayne went to Saratoga for the summer. I went to Ellis Park and won a few races for him there. In the fall of 1994 the Breeder's Cup was at Churchill Downs, so Wayne came back to Louisville. Pat Day didn't want to ride the fall meet; he had been working hard all summer and had decided to sit out the fall meet and ride at Keenland in October.

Basically, Wayne told his assistant in Kentucky that he was going to go ahead and give me a shot at the Turfway Meet and see how it worked out. They didn't tell me I was going to ride all the horses, but I was getting all the calls. I rode eleven horses at the meet; ten of them won. Needless to say, for me it was back to God having a hand in everything. The one horse of the eleven that didn't win and ran fourth, we won with at Keenland. This really helped me get in with the barn. If only five of the eleven had won, Pat Day would have been back on every one of them at Keenland in October. When it came to the Stakes Races, I rode the horse entered with Pat Day's horse for the barn, instead of the trainers going to the second leading rider in the standings.

I won many times, including some stakes races, for Wayne on a horse named Lost Pan. Lost Pan was the underdog a race in which Pat Day was riding the favorite for Wayne. This win started to give me credibility with a lot of the owners for whom Wayne trained. Lost Pan was preentered in the Breeder's Cup with me up, but the field was way too full for him to get in with

As I won stakes races for D. Wayne Lukas on horses like Golden Attraction, I saw my dreams turning into realities.
Courtesy of Barbara D. Livingston.

Great Women in the Sport of Kings

small earnings. That's when things started really to look good, and my life was just perfect. My life is still perfect, but that's when all my dreams started to become realities. I would pick up *Blood-horse* magazine and read "Donna Barton—Up and Coming" "Wow, did you see that?" I would say. I rode a filly named Cat Appeal in the Breeder's Cup that year. She didn't win there, but I did win a few stakes races on her after that. The fall of 1994 was incredible; nothing went wrong.

My favorite horses that I've ridden, besides Lost Pan, are Lord Carson, Boone's Mill, and Cat Appeal. Country Cat is immortalized in my mind, and when she broke down, it broke my heart. I just loved her; she always seemed to come through just when I needed a horse to come through for me.

For a couple of reasons my career highlight was running second in the Breeder's Cup on Hennesey. I've never been happy to run second, but everyone was so happy for me, and the owner, Mr. Lewis, had so many nice things to say on national television about my ride. Hennesey ran a terrific race; he gave me 100 percent of whatever he had. He knew I needed it, and I feel he did it for me. And, of course, the winner Unbridled's Song, turned out to be a nice little horse in his own right. At the time I stood up and said, "Who's that piece of garbage that beat me anyway?" But looking back, everything was okay, and Hennesey is a beautiful horse.

Wayne has put me in so many good positions and put me on so many good horses. I named a few of my favorites, but there are at least seventy more. Just to have been able to work Serena's Song and Timber Country, Thunder Gulch, and Grindstone, and to play a part in the development of their careers has been a great feeling. Wayne always makes me feel part of those victories when the horse wins the next race after I've worked him.

Another thing that has been great about riding for Wayne is that when I'm down about running second or not winning and I go by the barn and I still can't find what I did wrong or a reason during the race for not winning, Wayne will say to me, "Donna, every time we lose, we lose together. It's a team effort." He's the same way with his other riders, like Gary Stevens, Pat Day, and Jerry Bailey. When I ride for Wayne, I am riding for "Team Lukas"; I'm not out there by myself. He trusts me; whatever I do out there is fine. If it doesn't work out, I come back and talk about it with him and do something different the next time. He's really great to ride for.

In 1996, I broke the record at Churchill Downs for the most races won by a female rider. I broke my own record from the year before by two. I won four races on one day, June 28, which is the same day I closed on my house. People say, "Aren't you happy, this is what you've been shooting for?" I feel it's just like climbing stairs. When I get to the top of the stairs, yes, every step represents a victory, but there is another flight of stairs right there to climb. The best is yet ahead of me.

Favorites, Fans, Friends

My home has been a big project for me. I bought it on June 28, 1996, and I've done a lot of work on it. I've enjoyed every bit of it. I always have a lot of projects going on. Right now, I'm learning how to use my computer. I'm taking a course on the Silva method of learning. I just finished

Donna Barton

a course on accelerated learning techniques. I'm reading two different books, watching a movie, and listening to an audio-book by Joseph Campbell right now. I average three thousand miles a month on my truck. I have a set of books, "The World's 100 Greatest People," in one hundred volumes and "The World's 100 Greatest Books" on tape, so while I'm driving I listen to those. I always have one project, if not five, going on. I love musicals. I don't go out to a lot of movies. I used to play golf and volleyball, but with riding I don't need the physical release most people who work, let's say, in an office would need.

Now that I've reached my thirties, I like to keep more in touch with people from my childhood and people I've met through the years. I've learned how to use my e-mail. I'm much better about sending birthday cards and thank-you cards than I used to be. I try to maintain friendships now; they are important. When I was a kid, everybody was my friend, but when I got older, I realized that I had few very good friendships and it's important to let them know I think of them that way.

I have a great boyfriend now. In the past whenever I had a boyfriend and my sister approved of him for me, she would say to him, "Don't bug her. Don't ask her out tomorrow and the next night and the next night! In about four days she's going to be sick of you." My sister and my mother are my best friends even though I also hang out with other people. I talk to my brother out in California twice a week sometimes for an hour at a time. It's a really good feeling to be friends with people who will never betray me and never judge me. It's hard to find that loyalty outside my family, but Julie Krone and I have that kind of friendship. I have a lot of friends whom I value but don't get to spend a lot of time with. I don't like to talk on the phone, but I wind up spending a lot of time on the phone anyway!

I get fan mail, mostly from people who send me the jockey trading card with my picture on it, wanting it signed and returned to them, and letters saying, "I'm your biggest fan," and things

From *left to right:* my sister Leah, my brother Jerry, me after winning the Gardenia Stakes aboard Country Cat at Ellis Park in 1996, and my mom, Patti Barton-Brown, one of the pioneer female jockeys in our sport. *Courtesy of Suzie Picou, Oldham Photography.*

Great Women in the Sport of Kings

along those lines. I always write back to those who write me, and I greatly appreciate those who do, but I can't get into a pen-pal situation, and sometimes that is what people expect.

Riding in the state of Kentucky is amazing. I was on a 3:5 shot and ran second. I didn't look happy coming back after the race, and someone said, "Donna, don't look so sad. You'll be alright. The next one will run better." Only in Kentucky! Can you imagine that happening in New York or Florida? Never. People here are so nice. Why should I ever leave here? I have no traffic as I drive to work, and the license plates have the "twin spires" and horses on them. What could be wrong with that? One day a guy in the crowd at the track was standing next to where the trainers stand before the race. One of the trainers asked who he was betting on, and he said, "Sugar Britches." "Who's that?" the trainer asked. "Donna Barton," he replied. So for a year I was "Sugar Britches" to all the trainers. Better that then some other words, I thought. Kentucky fans are just the greatest.

The Path

So many people are driven by what has been ingrained in them about what they can and cannot accomplish—what is or isn't possible for them because they are women or from Chicago or only five-feet tall. So many people have so many dreams that they don't even try to realize because they just don't think they can do it. Unless they think they can do something, they can't. But I do know I can do whatever I set my mind to doing and I can accomplish a great many things as long as I think I can accomplish them and I set out to do them. I have to have a goal, and I have to be persistent. I have to have single-mindedness of purpose and accept nothing less than I set myself to do. Any negative feedback I get from people is fine; I pay no attention because they are not living my life. Any inventors anybody can name failed fifty thousand times before they got to their objectives. Babe Ruth, who set the record for home runs, struck out more times than he hit home runs. Everybody who has been famous or known for something suffered more failures and losses and disappointments along the path to that greatness than he did greatness. People should learn to accept mistakes and failures as learning lessons.

My advice to girls who are thirteen, fourteen, and up who want to ride and come up against people who say they're not strong enough or as strong as the guys is to keep the following think-ing in mind: comparisons like that are all well and fine if they are talking about the difference between a cheerleader and a football player. But they're talking about athletes who are the same size. If I weigh 100 lbs. and that guy weighs 100 lbs., I'm going to be just as strong if not stronger. When it comes to riding horses and winning races, I use my head a lot more than I use my arms or my whip, and I can't see any reason why gender should even be a factor as far as being a jockey is concerned. I can see why basketball, football, or baseball isn't going to open up to women anytime soon because women for the most part aren't that big and tall, but jockeys are all the same size.

I think that parents should want only good things for their kids and want for them what makes them happy. I think if a child has a parent who is not supportive of her serious career ambi-

Donna Barton

tions to become a jockey or an equestrian jumper or a lawyer, she should reevaluate her relationship with her parents and realize that even though her parents think they have her best interest in mind, it may not be what's best for her. There comes a point when she must look inside her soul and see what she wants to do and get in touch with that. If she weighs the pros and cons and horse racing keeps coming up as the choice, she must follow and trust her intuition. If her parents love her, they're going to support her anyway. If after a lot of hard work and dedication on her part, they do not stand by her, then they weren't going to stand by her back when she decided not to do what they wanted her to do. So she might as well go ahead and break free and cut the cord. She must follow her intuition.

Girls can start riding as jockeys at sixteen, but if girls' parents do not support them, they'll have to wait until they're eighteen and free to make those decisions. But they can work toward their goal from an early age. They can start riding and working around horses. I started race riding when I was twenty-one, but I remember working and getting paid when I was ten years old to tend to some horses. Paula Keim-Bruno started riding as a jockey at age thirty. In my mother's time Sandy Schleiffers, a nun, left the convent because of her earlier love of riding horses. My mother had three kids before she ever rode her first race.

I would like to say to all the girls and women out there who think they might want to ride to do it well or don't do it at all. It does the population of female riders no good to have bad female rider representatives; in fact, it's embarrassing. We are riding and working hard to knock down barriers to prove we are good and "as good as the guys." I've even had some owners whose wives haven't come to realize that women riders are good and have kept me off mounts, so the discrimination that still exists isn't just from men. Some women think if a woman wants to be a jockey it's for some ulterior motive, not riding. It's hard to believe. More and more women are sticking together and supporting one another because they know it was so hard for so long for women to move forward and get to where they wanted to go. Success at any level is a state of mind, and if I hadn't thought I was going to achieve what I did, I wouldn't have. If I had thought I was finished I would have been, but I'm not and I have a lot of great things ahead of me and I intend to do them.

Kristi Chapman (center). *Courtesy of Kristi Chapman.*

Kristi Chapman

Kristi is the youngest of the top female jockeys, barely in her midtwenties. Born and raised in Ohio, she considers Florida home. Her dad, brother, and sister are all in the Thoroughbred horse business. Full of talent and already with a lot of riding accomplishments in her budding career, she tells her story in a language that teenagers, young adults, and the kid in everyone can relate to. She is an outstanding role model of how positive direction in the formative years of life can produce early success and be a blueprint for a life with good self-esteem.

In addition to many win, place, and show credits Kristi developed a name for herself as a jockey who was able to get horses out of the starting gate in excellent condition and position. She can always get a horse to relax—a plus before a race. She communicates the easiness she has with herself to her mounts and has brought horses with odds of more than 40:1 to the winner's circle.

Eighty-eight Acres of Horses

I was born and raised in Norwalk, Ohio. I went all the way through high school living there except in the winters when we would go down to Florida. My father was a trainer at Thistledown Racetrack in Cleveland. My brother rode as a jockey there, too, and also a little bit in Florida. So, early on, I got a taste of being involved with horses and the racetrack.

Our farm in Ohio was for sale during the three years before I finished high school. It was eighty-eight acres and full of horses. Just before I graduated, it sold. Things were totally meant to be. Two weeks after graduation Mom sent me to Florida saying, "Dad needs your help." Dad, Jim Chapman, was in Florida at Calder Racetrack with thirty head of horses. My brother was there, too. It was right after Hurricane Andrew. There was no racing for one week, and my brother had gotten a little heavy; he always had to fight weight. He quit riding three weeks later and went out to California to work.

Dad put me on my first race horse to gallop. I always wanted to gallop. I had never gone to my dad about it because my mom had said, "No, no, you can't do it." She said that because my sister had died in a horse accident, and she was scared for me. I was the baby of six kids, and she didn't want me to risk being injured.

My brother actually helped me up on my first racehorse to gallop before he left. I started with a really large horse and galloped her for one month. Then dad put me on a couple of other horses that were easier. I wound up riding as a jockey ten months after that. It was a very quick transition for me. I had shown horses when I was in school and had ridden ever since I was little, but it was different getting on a racehorse .

My father hadn't always been a horse trainer; he had done other things before I was born. My older sister, who is sixteen years older than I am, told me he had had a trucking company but still had managed to own a few horses even back then. We moved to the farm one town over from where I was born when I was four, so all I ever knew were the horses, the horses. My other sister's fatal accident happened one year before I was born. She was nine years old. My mom saw it all. My mother didn't have a fear of me riding when I was little because she saw how natural it was for me, but she did have a fear of me riding races. It was the potential of injury that didn't sit well with her.

I always dreamed about being a jockey when I was little. When I was in high school and ran horses down to the racetrack at Thistledown for my dad, I could feel it. I wanted to ride. I knew I could do it, but I had never even galloped at that point and had no base to build a reality. So my dad never knew of my desire, only my mom. I told my brother, "I want to gallop, I want to ride," and he would just laugh at me.

When I arrived in Florida after high school and my brother was still there before leaving for California, I made him take me out on one of the ponies. He came back and told my dad, "She's alright." It went on from there.

I didn't know anything about riding style. I just watched my brother ride, and it didn't register in my head as anything but, "Oh, that's my brother doing it." I watched horses. I had horses as role models. Genuine Risk was the first one I admired, and there were many more after her.

Becoming a Jockey Was a Natural Progression

I had help from a couple of people when I started riding. Jacinto Vasquez was in Florida at the time and riding for my father. He was a good friend of mine and helped me a lot. Unfortunately, he was seriously injured shortly after that. Mary Russ, who was in the jockey's room with me most of the time, was a great teacher and a great friend. When Julie Krone and Donna Barton came down to Gulfstream Park in the wintertime, they gave me pointers and helped me with my riding also.

The racetrack was always my family's life. I didn't have to choose it for myself, but I love the horses. I love all animals, and it was a natural progression for me. As I was growing up, I brought a couple of close friends to the races once in a while, and my brother had his friends there watching him ride. That was neat. All my friends knew it was my life, and they accepted it. It was more fun for them to come out to my farm because we had golf carts and animals and all sorts of things to play around with. I always looked in the newspaper to see when my brother would ride because I didn't want to be at school, I wanted to be at the races.

My parents were strict with us. We weren't allowed to go out a lot and stay out late, but that was fine with me because I wanted to be with the animals anyway, and we had lots of animals. I didn't have to go out to the mall or partying to see my friends; they were very happy to come out and see me. Horses were the ones to steal my heart; I just loved them so much.

I don't personally own any horses now because I'm riding all the time. Jockeys aren't allowed to own racehorses. I could have a show horse or a riding horse, but I don't have the time to take care of it properly.

When I rode in Florida, I worked horses in the morning also. Certain horses I did really well with and would get on them all the time. I was very attached to them. Some horses are really responsive. I'm riding mostly in Kentucky now, and I'm on horses in the morning that really make my day. I love my work.

My dad is still in Florida. He's working on his pilot's license now. He actually has the license, but he's trying to upgrade it. My brother is in California and training horses on his own and doing well at Hollywood Park. He's a good horseman; he learned well from my father. He has twelve to fourteen horses in his barn, and they are all running.

All my jobs while growing up were with my family. I never had to take any outside jobs because there was always something to do; we had so many horses. I went right from high school to the racetrack with Dad. My parents always took good care of us. My mother is finally getting over her fear of me riding racehorses. In fact, she told me she is more comfortable with me riding now than she was when my brother was riding. She is also glad I don't have a problem with my weight. I've always been 102 lbs. at the most. She has realized that this is what I love and want to do. I've explained to her, "Mom, I'm going to be honest with you. I know this sounds bad, but I would rather be hurt or killed in a horse accident while doing what I'm loving doing than be shot somewhere or be crossing the street and get hit. Just let me do what I love to do and let me go if something happens." My mom actually likes to watch me ride now since I've been doing so well.

I still consider Florida and Calder Racetrack my home because even though I didn't grow up there, my riding life started there and I did great there. I did win my first $100,000 race here in Kentucky, and I'm going to ride in Kentucky for one year and decide where to go after

In the walking ring at Gulfstream Park Racetrack aboard Cielo Song. *Courtesy of Kristi Chapman.*

Kristi Chapman

that. I love Kentucky; there are so many horsemen here. It's been a challenge and exciting at the same time. My sister also lives here, and I'm happy to be here with her.

They All Noticed

My first ride as an apprentice jockey was amazing. I won! I won the first time out in the feature race of the day. It was on a filly that I had galloped in the morning. She was kind of a funny filly. She was fast; she could run, all right. My brother had broken her as a maiden, but she was very bad in the starting gate. She was improving by the time I got to ride her. My dad was going to start me on another filly on the turf, but she was a "nut case." So he put me on Pancho's Choice, and it worked out great. I knew her. Dad thought it would be perfect because I would not be permitted to carry a stick the first time I raced and she didn't like to be hit. Dad knew we were just great together. It was a six furlong race, and we won. I was nineteen. I rode her on June 18, 1993, at Calder. All this happened quickly in my life, I thought; I had just graduated from high school in June 1992. My first ride and my first win, wow! I felt safe on her because I knew her so well. There we were coming down the stretch, and were in the lead. I had practiced so many times in the morning, but it wasn't the same. I visualized what was going to happen in that race, and it actually happened the way I visualized it. Races don't always go like that, but it did for us that day. She dug in and we won. I was so happy for my dad, who had trained her, and for Arthur Appleton, who owned her.

After my first win, I didn't ride for a couple of weeks. When I started back, they let me have the whip because I did well in my first race. It was horrible; I couldn't hit a horse. It wasn't until three months after I started back riding that I knew what to do with the stick and could "switch sticks" in midrace. I was bad with the stick in those early months, but I was good at "rating" horses, which means judging their timing and position in a race, and horses broke really well for me from the gate. I was known for how horses excelled out of the starting gate with me after a time. I was always able to get a horse to relax.

After a while, I started riding really well. Dad had great horses and put me on them. I kept winning. Most of the wins came during the Tropical Meet at Calder in November–December. I was really improving and was leading "bug" rider. I had won my first handicap race there, beating a Shug McGaughey horse at the wire on Pancho's Choice, my dad's filly once again. I was feeling great and knew God had blessed me. I look back at all the wins I had there, and it was just amazing.

When I go through a slow time in my career, it's comforting to look back at my accomplishments. I learn a lot when it's slow, like patience, for instance. Then sometimes I just click with someone or a situation. I remember riding for Harold Rose in Florida. He eventually rode me on his whole stable because the first four horses he put me on at Hialeah Racetrack I won on, and we came from dead last. They were all long shots. He had faith in me. If I didn't win on horses during the first or second ride, he still rode me back on them. Other trainers would most likely have switched riders, and I would have missed the win when the horse got good, but not Mr. Rose; he was wonderful. I learned everything about each of his horses; I would tell him things, and we would work on them. We were great together. We won a stakes race with a horse named Mia's Hope. I can't say enough nice things about the Roses; they really took me under their wing. I was like their child. I keep in contact with them; I won't find a relationship like that in racing very often. I'm so lucky to know them, and I really miss them.

I actually started riding for Harold Rose at the end of my apprenticeship. I mostly rode my father's horses at first although my fifth win came on a horse trained by Angel Medina, who liked to give "bug" riders shots. When I started winning, winning, winning all the time, other trainers started to give me a chance. The fact that I was a woman was never an issue at all, especially in Florida. When owners and trainers have the opportunity to watch someone ride for a while they can see her ability and love for the horses. Gender doesn't come into it when they know her and her work.

Horses Are My Family's Love and My Life

How long can I envision myself riding? Well, I'm the kind of person who doesn't plan ahead too much. I like to take one day at a time. I don't think I will ever be away from the racetrack, though, in one way or another. Training horses like my brother and father do is definitely a possibility later. One thing I do know is that I will never be without horses and animals in my life. My sister is training horses in Kentucky now. I always will be "hands on" with horses in some capacity; that's a definite.

Injury is not something I think about; in fact, I block it out. I can't focus on it even if something does happen to me or to another rider. I can't ride a race with fear in my mind. The horses

Spending time with one of my favorite horses, Wire Me Collect. We've won together a lot and like spending time with each other.
Courtesy of Kristi Chapman.

Kristi Chapman

sense fear, and I would ride a bad race. Riders just have to relax and that is something that comes naturally to them now or they wouldn't still be here. Jockeys who are rattled by fear don't make it in their careers as riders.

I'm really "mushy" about the horses I ride, even the ones that I don't know well. People laugh at me, but I know my communication with the horses works. There's nothing wrong with sensitivity. One horse in particular that I used to ride for Mr. Rose put her head in between my legs in the paddock all the time. Everyone would laugh and she would just win, win, win.

I would like to see more people come to the live races. The racetracks where the weather is good all the time and certain meets attract a lot of people. I think if the racetracks did more things like family days and other little activities at the track for kids, they would draw more people. At Arlington Park they had a stand up cutout of jockey Gary Stevens and a hole next to him to put your face in on a horse and have your picture taken. Fun things like that attract people and promote racing, especially when they're free.

I think a major factor in becoming a jockey is a natural feeling for animals and I hope young girls recognize that in themselves. Jockeys' formost job is to communicate with the animals and to know how to talk to people also. A good personality and confidence helps, but girls need to start at the bottom and work their way up as in anything else. I was totally blessed because I had the opportunity to do that right in my own backyard from the time I was a child, but I went through all the stages by cleaning stalls and grooming horses, nevertheless. Unless a girl can ride like Angel Cordero at age sixteen, she can't just walk in and say, "I'm going to be a jockey," and jump on a horse. She will have to understand that it will take time. She will have to be humble and mean it. If it's in her heart to be a jockey, she won't mind starting from the bottom.

My dogs: Taylor, my Rottweiler,
and Angel, my bulldog.
Courtesy of Kristi Chapman.

Great Women in the Sport of Kings

Lessons

I was always athletic in school, especially in track. I was a freshman on the senior relay team, so I was a quick little thing. I never worked out when I was younger and only do so now when I'm bored. I really get all the exercise I need riding and working horses. I've never had a weight problem. When I rode in Florida, I was 101 lbs, really light; now I'm about 107 lbs. I'm learning to eat better now because I love "junk" food, and I know I can't do that forever. Donna Barton and Julie Krone would come into the jockeys' room, and I would be eating hamburgers and all that kind of stuff. They would say, "Kristi, that's going to catch up with you eventually." I would think, "Yeah, right." Well, not that I'm heavy or over the required weight, but I did put on a few pounds after being very light. Now when they see me, they say, "See, I told you!" It was a good lesson for me because I'm learning to eat healthily. God gives me trials all the time, and I learn really quickly. It's exciting to watch how things work out; everything happens for a reason.

I've cut out eating cakes and doughnuts. I eat vegetables now, whereas I paid no attention to them before. Thank God, I've always loved water. I always took vitamin supplements and continue to do so. I used to sit and eat a whole cake in one day, but now I'm eliminating all that garbage from my diet. I'll have a few cookies once in a while, but that's it.

What do I do in my off time from the track? I sleep. When I was in Florida, it was like home to me, so I would go to the movies by myself and I would go to certain restaurants and everybody would know me. I wouldn't mind being alone because I had ridden the card; I was tired and actually just wanted to be by myself. I like being around people but the more people, I'm around, the quieter I become. I let very few people into my life on a personal level. I don't trust everybody, but I will give everybody a shot. So, basically, I stay by myself. I go out once in a while. I don't like dating. If there is somebody I like, I take the time to see what develops. I never went out a lot back in my school days either. I'm not a "party animal," but I'm a bubbly person, so I have fun with anything I do. I don't like being tired in the morning, which is another reason why I don't go out too much.

I'm very dedicated to what I do, my work. I love to do 110 percent. I love getting up in the morning. In Florida I would get up at 4:30 A.M. because the training track opened at 5:00 A.M.; the main track opened at 5:30 A.M. I'd be up rolling in the dark; I loved it. I thrive on getting out of bed and getting out there on the track. It's my favorite time of the day to be with the horses.

Sometimes I think about what it would be like to be out there in the world having to do what everybody else does. I get very depressed thinking that, and it makes me want to cry. When I first started riding, I didn't want to hear anything other than racing and the racetrack. I was scared to death even to be away from the racetrack, I loved it so much. It was like I was in a dream and going to come out of it if I thought about anything else. Now I'm a little more "normal." I feel settled in my life. I'm not scared the wonderful dream is going to stop.

I get along with most people. I mind my own business and mostly stay to myself. I get along with my coworkers, both male and female. I don't run into sexist stuff too much. I hear

Kristi Chapman

about it sometimes at the smaller tracks. I think it's probably a "macho thing" where the guys don't want the girls coming in and beating them, but where I ride I don't experience it. I get fan mail. If it's from kids, I especially like it. I've been on the jockey trading cards for two years now and sometimes I will get the one I'm on in the mail with a request to autograph it and send it back. I do that and also sign a lot of them in person when people come with them to the track.

I realized a lot of my immaturities when I started riding professionally. I knew I had to get rid of them. I'm still a kid; I'm still learning. I'm really blessed that I see my mistakes quickly and don't go back to do them again. Patience is a big thing, and I'm still working on it in riding and in life. When I have time on my hands, I think a lot. I know there are things I can have now and things in my life I will have to wait for, but I believe in God and I really trust in Him. Whatever goes on in my life is for a reason. I used to get depressed and down when things weren't happening when, where, and how I thought they should. Now I'm at ease and happy with any circumstance because I'm confident there is a reason for everything. I've enjoyed learning that lesson; it's made me a better person.

And Then Came Julie

Julie Krone has been the greatest friend and a generous helper along with Donna Barton. Sometimes I feel as if I'm their baby sister. Other people can attest to this about Julie; there is "something" about her. She has an amazing mind and heart. I, of course, knew about the great success of Julie Krone, but when I really got to know her and rode side by side with her and we talked and related to each other, I really understood why she is such a successful person and rider. As a rider, she is tops. She can communicate with the horses like I've never seen anybody do before. She can get into a horse's mind. When she came to Gulfstream, that was my "battery charge" to go on for the rest of the season. I thrived on seeing and watching her. I can't explain in words what she does and what she does for me. She is just amazing. She points out things in riding and in life that I would never think to think of. She refreshes me. It's been a great opportunity to be around the great Julie Krone but an even greater gift just to be around Julie.

Donna Barton's a great person, too. She is so wonderful and so professional. It was basically the three of us in the jockey's room at Gulfstream when I started riding; Julie, Donna, and me. I was very immature as a rider and as an individual, and they felt for me and wanted to help me. They were great. I listened to them then, and I listen to them still. They have watched me come along professionally and personally, and I've been so glad to have them as role models and friends.

Mary Russ was my first role model. She has quit riding now to be with her family, but she was amazing, too. Mary was such an aggressive rider. She was better than any of the male riders. She was strong, a bull! She was a good-hearted, person, a family-oriented person. A lot like Julie, she could communicate with the animals and find their special qualities easily. She was a great rider. I didn't try to copy her style, but I surely did admire her. She was there for me and gave of herself more than 100 percent. One day I hope I'll be able to help an up-and-coming rider like those wonderful women helped me. Riding and the people I have met through riding have taught me and will continue to teach me about myself and continue to enrich my life. Being a jockey has opened me up as a person. I am forever grateful to the horses and to the people who love them and have loved me.

Kristi Chapman

Dodie Duys (left). *Courtesy of Tom Pellegrino.*

Dodie Duys

Dodie grew up in a family of exceptional athletes with the desire to excel bred into her. She built a career as a jockey despite having to spend a lot of time defending herself against what she considered injustice born of the jealousies of her male rivals. Standing firm behind her own talent, good form, and determination, Dodie has ridden all over the world and now enjoys successful riding meets in Florida and New England.

Dodie's riding style, great communication with the horses, and respect from the trainers consistently produce wins for all concerned. Statistically, Dodie has been in the top ten standings at every riding meet, including those in her early days at the Fairgrounds in Louisiana. When she rode in Japan in 1992, Japanese reporters stated she was the best female rider they had ever seen.

It Was in the Breeding

I was born and raised in Quincy, Florida, which is a really nice, old Southern town. It's the second oldest town in Florida. My dad was a tobacco farmer, so naturally, I was in the country quite a bit. At first we had a house in town right across from the park, so when the other kids wanted to play baseball and football, they called for the three Duys kids. I was kind of a tomboy, so my sister and I were included with the guys. My brother was the oldest of us three; I was the youngest, and I had to learn to keep up with them all the time. We were all one year apart, but I did a good job of keeping up with them.

Everyone in our whole family was a very exceptional athlete, and we knew it when we were very young and started competing from the time we were six years old on. Both my parents were incredible athletes and very smart people. My dad was an All American soccer player, and there were trophies all over the house. It's funny just how much is bred into people—just like what is bred into racehorses: the competitive nature, the desire to excel and to be the best. Fortunately, some smarts were bred into us, too. My mother was called the "encyclopedia"; there weren't computers back then. She is amazing. She can memorize everything that she is told. She is audiogenic, whereas my memory is more photogenic. Whether it's house plans or a horse, in my memory it's as if I had just looked at it. I can tell you years later everything about that horse, including his quirks. I wish I had my mom's memory with people's names, but, thank goodness, I can remember their faces.

I remember being very competitive already at six years old, winning a ribbon by jumping horses. I looked like a peanut up on the horse; I have a picture at home in Quincy, and you can see my helmet is too big and is falling off. All of us rode in my family. We all fox hunted. We all have our colors with the Midland Foxhounds. My parents and I have our colors with the Live Oak Hounds also. These are both extremely good fox hunts. Fox hunting was a family thing we did on the weekends. As a family we also did a lot of water-skiing and played a lot of tennis. My sister really excelled as a tennis player and had a scholarship to Auburn University for volleyball. She was also good at racquetball and has about forty trophies from different tournaments that she has won. I have my big stack of trophies and, of course, they are all "horsey."

I was raised to think I should go to college. It was an expected thing in the Duys family. Everyone in our family, generation after generation, has gone to college. I came up a little short. I took a summer job during college down in Miami and saw the kind of money jockeys were making and realized I could do the weight. I also realized I was a good enough rider and just had to learn what jockeys do as compared to jumper riders. I was twenty-two and in my third year of college at Auburn, studying architecture. Back then it was a very prestigious school. I was in landscape architecture, which I loved; I loved plants and still do. Landscaping involves horticulture, architecture, and engineering, which was a breeze because I'm mostly German. I was forced in college to get away from riding horses. I didn't like that; I felt like part of my life was missing without the horses. It was a big battle. I was afraid of bringing my horse up to school because I knew I would spend too much time with her, taking care of her.

I bred my horse and wound up getting some really nice foals from her. She's still up at my parent's home in Quincy in good health and looks beautiful. We had her mother for thirty-six years that we know of, and my horse is getting close to thirty now and looks absolutely fabulous. She and I were like one spirit together. She is a white mare named Novelty, half Thoroughbred and half Arabian and Quarter Horse mixed. We used to win all our steeplechase races together. That was so much fun, and I think that is where I got the "little disease" of liking racing. I also fox hunted on her, won all my open jumping on her, and did some three-day-eventing and dressage with her. She could run fast and jump high.

Destiny Prevails

I think no matter what course one takes, one winds up doing what one is destined to do. My first job out of high school was with a man on Hobo Farm, learning about Thoroughbred racehorses. I didn't have a car, so it was great that I could live on a farm. Three months later I went off to college, but I felt so much love and desire for horses, one way or another they were going to be part of my life. I love competing; some people just do. I was good at competing with horses. If I wasn't good at it, I wouldn't have pursued it.

Friends with whom my family and I fox hunted got me started with some of the top steeplechase outfits in the country. I did ride pretty well in the hunt meets and although I don't like to sound as if I'm bragging, it was obvious I had a lot of natural talent. I looked into some of the statistics about steeplechase riders and found that during one of every ten rides a steeplechase rider will go down. I had gone to see the Atlanta Steeplechase every year since I was four years old and had seen some riders get killed. I saw a lot of them get hurt and thought pretty seriously about whether to get into it professionally.

I missed the horses so much. I enjoyed architecture, but I didn't love it. I decided not to go on with steeplechase riding. I knew riders who were pretty banged up. I knew a fabulous rider who had had so many concussions he couldn't even talk right.

My next summer job after the Hobo Farm work was breaking and training horses in Alabama. I helped put myself through school with that job. All the horses that I worked with went up to Finger Lakes Racetrack and broke their maidens first time out. I was pretty impressed with that record except that I had expected to be on them. I wanted to ride as a jockey then, but the owner was afraid I would get hurt. He wanted me to be a trainer, but I knew I wasn't ready for that. I was good at conditioning, but not at training; I wasn't good with all the medications and dealing with the people and knowing where to run a horse.

I went back to college and finished my third year although I had a hard time earning enough money to do that. I met a friend of mine, Jonathan Jordan, while partying at FSU, which is right next door to Quincy, Florida. He said I could go down to Miami and stay with his parents in Kendall in South Miami. Mr. Whaley, my boss, knew I wanted to start riding and also knew I didn't have transportation. He helped me get a VW "Bug." He was so nice, such a gentleman; he sent me twenty-five hundred dollars to get that car.

In Miami I started to work for Jimmy Bracken and galloped horses for other people. I looked terrible riding; I looked like a steeplechase rider at first, but I knew I could manage anything. I could handle a horse and make him do anything I wanted. I needed to look like a jockey on a horse. Even as an apprentice rider, I had a lot of trouble breaking myself of steeplechase habits to get into race riding style. I did gallop all of Jimmy Bracken's horses, including the tough ones. Even today, I get on all the tough horses for my husband and leave the easy ones for the exercise rider.

Mr. Bracken had promised to get me started riding as a jockey. I had left his barn for a while to work for other people. I learned a lot doing that, but Mr. Bracken was really the one who taught me almost everything. He let me work all the horses in his barn for well over a year and really helped me learn timing. He said this was the most important thing for a jockey to know, that is, how fast he or she was going. He would make me tell him the time on all the fractions of the race, the first quarter, the last three-eighths, and so on, as well as the final time. It was tough on me then, but I'm grateful for it now. I remember he used to make me cry a lot; it was really hard, but I wanted to learn the right way. I've always wanted to be the best at whatever I did. Mr. Bracken was the same way.

At this point I told my parents I wasn't going to put myself through school anymore; I was going to stay in Miami with my job. There wasn't a whole lot they could say; they had only paid for one year of my college and didn't want to continue. I became the black sheep of the family for a long time. I was expected to be a "professional" person. My brother and sister both had masters degrees. Even though my parents loved horses, the racetrack and the people they thought hung around the racetrack weren't whom they wanted me to be with.

Dodie Duys

Quite a variety of people are at the racetrack, just as anywhere else life takes me. I've met some of the finest people and the worst of the lowlifes. I rode in Japan for one month, and I was very impressed. The Japanese don't use any medications on their horses, and the horses seem to be more consistent. I was quite impressed with their whole system. When I finish my riding years, I think I would like to write a book on horse racing. It would be controversial just like my life and career have been.

She Can Horseback

Women still aren't accepted everywhere in racing. I noticed the farther west I went, the more chauvinistic men were about women competing with men as athletes. Their attitude was, "A woman can't do it because she has to be strong." Well, there is a lot more to racing than being strong. I'm quite strong and lucky for that, but jockeys have to be smart, quick, think quickly, have finesse with a horse, and know their timing to ride a racehorse. Men have always underestimated women as race riders.

```
                    CALLY HON
OWNER               SUFFOLK DOWNS        1 MILE
HARRIET C. HEUBECK                       DODIE C. DUYS
TRAINER             2ND. FUNNY FLASH     TIME 1:45.1
K.M.GRUSMARK        3RD. ITA KARINA      FEB. 21, 1993
```

Racing and winning in all weather conditions—unless the stewards declare the track surface unsafe, which happens occasionally.
Courtesy of Equi-Photo, Inc.

In so many barns in Louisiana when I walked in, they would say, "We don't ride girls," and I would walk right out. Next! Actually, I rode in Louisiana for the sweetest person I probably have ever met, Anitol Bourque. He should have been a politician; he was friends with everybody. He had about one hundred head of horses so I rode them at the Fairgrounds. How I got to Louisiana was interesting. I had quit riding because I wasn't getting a shot in Miami after I lost the "bug," my apprenticeship. I was on winners for Ralph Zadie; in fact, my claim to fame was that I was known as "Reggae Man's jockey." I seemed to have fans at the betting windows but needed them in the stable area. I'm a hard-trying rider, and I get a lot of run out of every horse I sit on. I don't play any games, and the public knows it. So how did I get to Louisiana? My mom and dad had bred some horses, and a partner and I bought two. We asked the racing secretary who would be a good trainer, not a high-profile type, but somebody who could get the job done. He recommended Anitol. He started to put me up on some horses. I won on some horses for him that paid a huge price.

I was a bit heavy then; I looked like a construction worker because I was doing some house painting to make money. I had to get my weight down. I did. Anitol was impressed by my riding. He is the fondest memory I have in racing. He was so good to me. He would let me off his horse if he thought his buddy had a better horse in the race that I could ride. He set me up with an agent and in general got things going for me. I have to give Randy Romero some credit here too. Randy was the top rider at Gulfstream when I was an apprentice. He was winning everything in sight, just "killin' em!" I loved to watch him ride; he was so smooth on a horse. He put a good word in for me with Anitol. Randy was from Louisiana, and when he came into town to ride horses for "fame week," he said, "Anitol, all this girl needs is a good shot. She can horseback." That really helped me a lot, and Anitol saw for himself that I was getting results.

I stayed in Louisiana. The trainers I was riding for loved me; the jockeys hated me. I was coming in and taking away their money; I guess that's how they saw it. I was just glad to be back in the saddle, and I was going to do the best I could for the people who hired me. I was an outsider who came in and won races. The other jockeys started to threaten me, but I passed it off as just being "hot under the collar." There was a lot of jealousy there, and it was the first time I ever had to deal with it on the extreme level. They liked to fight there; one of the first things I saw was the scuffling between them. I knew eventually it was going to be my turn; I could just sense it in the atmosphere. Someone did come at me, but we wound up not fighting; he backed off. Down the line I did have a couple of fights. I'm not proud of it, but I was doing nothing wrong on the racetrack. I was just winning, and the people who rode me liked that I didn't back down. I was my own person and did what I morally thought was the right thing to do.

The rulings were slapped on me for things I didn't do or say. I had to get a lawyer to straighten things out at Jefferson Downs. I won the case, and they reversed the rulings. I had a petition signed by 175 trainers and owners who stated it was jealousy that sparked those people into saying things in the first place and that I was of good character and tried to win on every horse I got

Dodie Duys

on. We brought in "neutral jockeys," the ones not part of the clique that was against me. I won the battle but not the war. I was severely injured in a race at the Fairgrounds. I was out of racing for a good while. My leg was shattered. I thought I was finished. I started to work on a hand-knotted rug of Mamalib crossing the finish line in which I used my skills to make the grid from a photo. I went back to architecture school, but I missed racing.

I started back at the Fairgrounds. My first day back I got on ten horses in the morning to work. After about two weeks of getting on as many horses as I could, I felt I was tight enough to ride. Hugh Carney came up to me and told me his brother was a major owner up at Rockingham Park and girls did well there. Why didn't I go up there? I had ridden some horses for Hugh at Fairgrounds. So I took him up on it, and he named me on some horses up there. He was the only one up there who knew how badly I had been hurt. He saw how much ability I had and that I wasn't being allowed to show it or to pursue my career.

I got an agent named Kurt Cartwright up there who handled girl jockeys; in fact, he had Diane Nelson. He was a really nice guy and got me started. I rode well and things started to happen for me there. I've ridden there for six years in the summer and will continue to do so. I would

Aboard Silvered Silk, ready to race.
Courtesy of Kriston Von Wise.

Great Women in the Sport of Kings

have been leading rider there during the last meet, but I got up there three weeks late and didn't get the jump on it. I rode Suffolk Downs but ran into jealousies from jockeys similar to those I encountered in Louisiana. One jockey in particular made it hard on me there, and things got into the newspaper about me that weren't true of my character. But last summer the same newspaper made amends by publishing a huge spread on me. They realized what had happened and saw I was the "good guy" instead of the "bad guy." I've had to be a crusader almost all because of being an honest, hard-trying rider who's female who could outride the local guys. I was winning on horses that didn't figure to win, beating these guys at the wire. The fact that I knew they had this attitude about me made me try all the harder to win. I was riding for trainers like Bill Perry, and the jockeys couldn't understand that; they thought I must be sleeping with him to get those mounts. I wasn't. It cost me a lot of business whenever they started rumors around the track like that.

I've still managed to keep riding, but I feel I haven't done what I should have, or could have, in my career. I've had to fight a lot of unfairness; but I tell you what, I've made one mark. My moral values are understood. I ride to win and that's it. I have a new agent now in Florida, and I feel it's a good partnership. He'll be with me at Rockingham Park in the summers, too.

The other good partnership in my life is with my husband. I knew him for a long time, but I didn't know him well. He's a trainer. His wife passed away from cancer four years ago. Gordon is a super person. It helps to be with someone who is in the same industry as I am. I've had past relationships that didn't work out because I was having to choose my career and traveling over my boyfriend. One thing I learned through all of it is that if a man is going to be loyal to me, if he wants to be loyal to me, no matter what, he will.

The Balance of Life

I've always wanted to be the leading female rider in the country. I felt I always had the ability to do that but never was given the chance. I don't necessarily feel it's too late, but at thirty-six, I feel a lot of my injuries when I ride. I'm very, very strong and certainly a lot smarter. I know what I'm doing out there, so if I'm going to become leading female rider, it's going to happen soon. I'm being realistic. Being leading rider has to do with who else is out there riding well and "hot" at the same time I am.

I've always been a really consistent rider and a consistent winner. I thought about riding over at Tampa, Florida, this year because I know I could do well there and accumulate a lot of wins but that would take me away from my home and my husband again. I've been away so much, Gordon wants me to stay here in Miami. It's always a struggle to balance a personal life with career moves.

Anyone reading this book should know there are tough situations in a personal life. When I was up in New England, all I did was eat, sleep, work, and work my hardest. I'm known as a really hard-working rider. I get on a lot of horses in the morning; I try to help everybody I ride for as much as I can. The only socializing I did was dinner once in a while with people for whom I worked.

Dodie Duys

117

Working toward becoming the leading female rider in the country. *Courtesy of Kate Chapman.*

I definitely got to a point in my life where I was losing a lot of the "meaning of life" itself because all I did was eat, sleep, and work seven days a week. Holidays I rarely got to go home. There was a big emptiness. When I met Gordon, there was a big emptiness in his life, too. He had lost a really good woman to cancer.

I never was keen on alcohol or going out partying all night. Two drinks were my limit if I was out socializing at dinner. If I want to be a good athlete, I can't mix in drinking or any kind of drugs. I've seen athletes who used drugs and alcohol and they thought they were "mighty men," but their judgment was really off and their minds were slow. In racing one has to be quick thinking, especially right out of the gate.

My mother is a dietitian, so I've always been careful and very conscious of what I eat. I do a lot of research on the latest findings about what my body needs. I read a lot of books on weightlifting training. I can get a lot out of that, but some I don't want. I put on muscle weight incredibly fast; it's genetic, so I have to be careful. I know my body really well and always have.

I used to swim. I built my lungs up so much over the years that I could swim three laps underwater in an Olympic-length pool with one breath. People still marvel about that. I did it many, many times; it wasn't just a freak thing. I had built myself up to that level. In high school I had the weightlifting record and still do. I could lift 720 pounds leg press. I yanked 500 pounds around as if it were nothing. I'd bounce the whole thing around and catch it just to show off. We had to lift weights for the volleyball team. I was short so I always rotated to the back, but I was a very good server. I was steeplechase riding at the same time all through high school. I also was taking ballet lessons. My leg muscles were tight! I couldn't do the splits in ballet but wound up doing a lot of modern dance routines. I was amazed when I pushed my body to the limits. I could also bicycle all day and never get tired.

In my career my happiest moments were when I rode in Japan. I've won stakes races in this country but nothing to equal the marks of Julie Krone winning the Belmont or Mary Russ being the first female to win a $100,000 race.

I was incredibly impressed with Japan's whole racing industry. We need to go over there and learn. They go to extreme measures to keep honesty in the sport. They don't use medications

Saying a prayer before my ride in one of the races in Japan.
Courtesy of Dodie Duys.
Photographer unknown.

Dodie Duys

on their horses like we do in America. People don't realize that medications can sometimes give a horse an edge in a race. The Japanese people rolled out the red carpet for us. We stayed at the finest hotels; they took us sightseeing and gave us three days in Tokyo with a translator, all expenses paid. Everything was very well organized, and I always knew what was expected of me.

We rode in four different cities at four different racetracks. The only mess-up that happened to me was when I won a race against their male jockeys on a long shot. I apparently whipped my horse too many times during the race. They frown upon too much use of the whip over there, but I rode that horse the same way I was used to riding here in America. They called me in, and I apologized. I thought there might be a whole set of rules over there that I wasn't aware of, but there wasn't; only the whipping was in question.

We rode a big variety of horses over there. I think that makes the competition equal because it tests our ability to ride lesser-quality horses and "good" horses as well. "Good" horses are much easier to ride. There were riders from different countries as well as from Japan. There were three riders from Japan and the girl rider who had won the challenge the previous three years lost to me the year I was there. The title of the meet was the World Female Competition. There were top female riders from Great Britain, France, Canada, two from the United States—Katie Sweeney and I—Australia, and, of course, Japan.

Every year the Japanese come over here and pick riders who have not competed before in this challenge and who are currently the best riders. But being away a whole month can kill your business here at home, so I know riders who were invited, like Diane Nelson, who chose not to go. They did want me to come back the following year to defend my title, but I was riding "first call" for a very important outfit, and we had some really nice stakes horses and I didn't want to give them up. I knew these horses would run well no matter who was sitting on their backs but they would run great for me.

I am very grateful to the Japanese for giving me an honest opportunity to compete on the same level as other riders. All the jockeys drew horses at each place we went in front of a whole auditorium of people and press. It was a random match up of jockey to horse. This was the first time I felt I was competing on completely the same level with other riders. I really liked that; it felt so fair. I didn't always have a "good horse," but part of the challenge was to make the most of what I had. This is what I do all the time anyway! I felt right at home. The whole meet was based on a point system, so even if I had finished fourth or fifth in a race, it could have made a difference in the final scoring. It made it important to do my best on every mount I sat on, which is how I ride anyway.

By the time I left Japan I could read the racing part, the past performances in the *Daily Racing Form* in Japanese because of the help of the interpreters. They actually got a kick out of the fact that I wanted to learn and got it right. We would "thumbs up" each other. This all happened in September 1992, and I can't say I could still read the form today and get it right, but it was an accomplishment then. If I were ever asked to go back to Japan, I would. I almost regret not going back the following year. Articles in the Japanese newspapers stated I was the best female rider they had ever seen. They awarded me a lot of money for my four wins and paid well for second and third place. I think I wound up making fifty thousand dollars plus tons of gifts and trophies. I was over there for one month with no expenses, not even for an agent or valet; everything was taken care of. I was so impressed by how genuinely courteous and polite the Japanese were to us and to each other even in big cities such as Tokyo. I thought, why can't we be like that in this country? It comes down to treating each other with respect and dignity.

Even though I'm aggressive in competition, I'm very shy when it comes to the business side of my racing career. It's part of my personaliy; I'm shy with people. I relate to horses beautifully and communicate with them as if I were a horse. I'm not such a good communicator with people. That's what I admire so much about Julie Krone; I feel her communication has a lot to do with her success.

I've been in the top ten rider standings at every meet, including back to my days at the Fairgrounds in Louisiana, but I want to be leading rider and the best rider, I want to get there.

Dodie Duys

Appendix
Glossary

Appendix

America's First Female Jockeys

Readers of this book should have some information on the women who opened the door for female riders back in the late 1960s to appreciate fully how far the Thoroughbred racing industry, the women, and the world have come. We honor the first female jockeys in America:

Kathy Kusner sued the state of Maryland in the mid-1960s and won the right to ride there but suffered a leg injury in a horse show at Madison Square Garden. She was an Olympic rider.

Penny Ann Early tried to race against male jockeys at Churchill Downs in Kentucky in the late 1960s only to encounter boycotts and name calling. After four attempts she gave up and played basketball for the Kentucky Colonels. She later obtained her jockey's license and rode in California.

Diane Crump rode on February 7, 1969, against male jockeys without too much trouble from them at Hialeah Racetrack, the first woman to do so.

Barbara Jo Rubin rode a horse to win at Charlestown Racetrack in late February 1969, making her the first female jockey and the first woman to win against men in any professional sport competition in American history. She appeared on the *Ed Sullivan Show* and the *Today Show*. She was nineteen years old at the time.

Tuesdee Testa rode at Santa Anita Racetrack in California and was the third woman in history to win a race at a Thoroughbred racetrack.

Sandy Schleiffers followed her love of horses and left a convent in which she was a nun in Clinton, Iowa, to become a jockey. At age twenty-three in 1970 she was the first woman ever to be admitted to the Jockey's Guild. Her first race was at Turf Paradise on March 2, 1969. She was the first woman in the history of the states of Arizona and Colorado to ride in and win a Thoroughbred horse race. She was the fourth woman in America to win a race. She is presently a college professor and is Dr. Sandy Schleiffers but likes it best when students call her "Dr. Jock."

Mary Bacon, a former Oklahoma cowgirl, jumped out of cakes topless and worked at other odd jobs before exercising horses and eventually riding. She obtained her jockey's license in May 1969 at Finger Lakes Racetrack in upstate New York. At age twenty-five she was one of the top female jockeys in America and had a daughter, Suzie, with her husband, jockey Johnny Bacon.

Cheryl White was the first black female jockey. She rode against Mary Bacon and other pioneering women in the late sixties and early seventies. She encountered no racial problems on the racetrack. She was one of the regular riders for pioneer woman horse trainer Beverly Cramer.

Claudia Weaver took on the objections of the wives of male jockeys to be allowed to change her clothes in the jockey's room. After his divorce from Mary Bacon she married jockey Johnny Bacon at Charlestown Racetrack on the finish line. It was a media frenzy.

Violet "Pinkie" Smith found it tough to make it as a jockey even though her dad was a horse trainer and she knew racetrack officials. She rode at Portland Meadows in Oregon and was the fifth woman to win a race at a Thoroughbred racetrack.

Robyn Smith was in 1973 the most well-known and glamorous jockey at the top racetrack in America, Aqueduct. Although she finished seventh in the jockey standings that year, the six men who finished ahead of her were all from other countries. She was 5'7" tall but only weighed 105 pounds. She originally obtained her jockey's license in 1969 at Golden Gate Racetrack but went to New York determined to hit the big time. She went straight to Belmont Park and persuaded trainers such as Allen Jerkens to put her up on their horses. She was married to Fred Astaire.

Donna Hillman was the daughter of actress Joan Barkley and was a former model for *Harper's Bazaar* magazine. She rode mostly in Maryland but did not like riding with the other women jockeys as much as she did with the men, even though she captured the My Fair Lady Handicap, finishing in first place.

Jennifer Rowland became Maryland's leading female jockey and sustained that title for many years. She just recently retired from racing.

Arline Ditmore was in 1973 one of the older female jockeys at age thirty-six. She rode and won quite frequently at Aqueduct Racetrack in New York. Riding at the time with her were jockeys Joan O'Shea, forty-seven, and Lillian Jenkens, who was in her sixties.

Linda Richmond and **Lois Meals** were identical twin female jockeys who, from humble beginnings as the daughters of Pittsburgh, Pennsylvania, schoolteachers, were able to make their livings as jockeys in the early 1970s.

Patti Barton-Brown grew up loving horses but with parents who did not. After high school, she rode bulls and broncos in the rodeo. After marrying cowboy Charlie Barton and having three children, she first rode as a jockey in 1969. Waterford Park Racetrack was her home track for most of her career. By 1971 she was the winningest female jockey in America. Her riding career ended with a spill in 1984 at age thirty-nine but her children, Leah, Jerry, and Donna Barton, went on to great heights in the Thoroughbred racing industry.

Patty "P. J." Cooksey is one of only a few female jockeys still riding at a major Thoroughbred racetrack who competed with some of the pioneer women jockeys such as the great Patti Barton-Brown. She paused in her long, successful riding career to have a baby and is now back riding in Kentucky.

Glossary

Allowance race: A race in which horses cannot be claimed by a new owner. Racetracks have a high-point price in claiming races; an allowance race is one step above that price. Certain conditions also are set: for example, a horse cannot have won two races in its lifetime or a specified monetary amount since a specific date.

Also eligible: In a field of horses a horse that will only run if a horse in the original lineup is scratched, or withdrawn, from the race.

Apprentice jockey: An inexperienced rider who is apprenticed for one year or thirty-five wins, whichever is longer, and is given considerable reductions in weight allowances on the horses he or she rides.

Backside: The stable side of the racetrack.

Bearing in (or out): In a race a horse moving inward toward the left, or rail, or outward toward the right, or outside.

Belmont Stakes: The third race in the Triple Crown series of races for three-year-old horses. It is run at Belmont Park Racetrack in mid-June.

Breaks down: A term that describes a horse that cannot finish a race because of sudden injury. A veterinarian assesses its condition; it usually has to be destroyed.

Breeder's Cup Day: Held in the fall at racetracks by rotation around the United States. It is the Olympics of horse racing with many different competitions, such as sprint races, long-route races, turf races, races for older horses, races for two year olds, and so on.

Bug: On the program at Thoroughbred racetracks to indicate the horse is being ridden by an apprentice jockey and is being given a weight allowance (extra weight reduction) to be able to compete in the same race with horses ridden by more-experienced jockeys.

Bleeder: A horse predisposed to bleed (hemorrhage) from the nostrils during a race or workout. Such bleeding can also appear immediately after such activity.

Blinkers: A hood with eyecups placed over a horse's head before it races. Blinkers prevent a horse from seeing distractions because it can only see straight ahead.

Breaking maiden: A horse winning its first race.

Breeze: When a horse gallops out to full speed without whipping or hard riding by the rider.

Brood mare: A female horse that has been bred to produce a foal.

Claiming race: A race in which horses of equal ability run but risk being claimed or bought out of the race by a new owner or trainer.

Clerk of scales: The person who checks the weights and equipment.

Colors: The bicolor shirt and cap, or jockey's silks, provided by the horse's owner.

Colt: A male horse five years or younger.

Condition: The eligibility rules and qualifications for a horse to be entered in a race.

Coupled entry: Two or more horses that run in a race as a single betting unit. They are owned or trained by the same person, and a bet on one is a bet on both.

Daily Racing Form: Newspaper giving statistics, news, and past performances of horses, jockeys, trainers, and owners.

Dam: The female parent of a horse.

Dark Day: The day the racetrack is closed to racing.

Dead heat: When two or more horses cross the finish line simultaneously.

Derby: A stakes race exclusively for three-year-old horses.

Equisizer: An exercise machine used by jockeys to simulate the workout they would get while riding a race or working a horse.

Filly: A female horse younger than five years.

Foal: A young horse of either sex in its first year of life.

Form: A horse running in peak physical condition.

Furlong: 220 yards; eight furlongs equal one mile.

Gate: Where race horses start to race no matter what the distance or surface.

Gelding: A castrated male horse of any age.

Groom: An employee who cares for the horses in the barn, feeds them, bathes them, and so on.

Handicap: A range of weights assigned by the racing secretary that should allow all the horses in a handicap race to finish simultaneously. The weights are also assigned according to a horse's past performance and present form.

Handicapper: A journalist or other official who assesses horses and races and reports his selections to the betting public.

Handily: A pace during a horse workout that is slower than driving but faster than breezing. This expression is also applied to a horse that wins a race with ease.

Hang: When a horse holds back to the pace of the horse next to him instead of forging ahead.

Head: A margin, the length of a horse's head, that describes the distance by which one horse leads another at the finish line.

Horse's birthday: January 1. For competitive purposes all horses become one year older on the same day each year.

Hot walker: A person who cools down a horse after its workout by walking it. It is also a mechanical device with four 40 ft. arms that is used to walk horses slowly after exercise.

Inquiry: An immediate investigation by the stewards at the racetrack into the running of the race. One or more horses may be disqualified as a result of their findings.

Irons: Stirrups into which jockeys and riders put their feet.

Journeyman: A licensed jockey who has completed his or her apprenticeship and is riding without any allowances different from those of other jockeys or weight reductions diffferent from those assigned to other horses.

Kentucky Derby: The most famous "two minutes in sports"—a stakes race for three-year-old horses always run the first Saturday in May at Churchill Downs in Louisville, Kentucky. It is the first race of the Triple Crown racing series.

Lane: The part of the track in front of the grandstand before the finish line, also called the homestretch.

Lasix: A brand name drug, furosemide. It is an antibleeding medication and diuretic that may affect a horse's performance in a race.

Lead pony: A horse that leads the racehorses from the paddock and walking ring to the starting gate.

Length: A unit of measure in horse racing and charting. One length is equal to the length of one horse. Five lengths are equal to the distance covered in one second at racing speed.

Lugging in (out): A horse pulling strongly to the inside or outside while running.

Maiden: A horse that has not won a race.

Maiden race: A race for horses that have not won.

Mare: A female horse five years or older.

Mudder: A horse that races well on a muddy track.

Neck: A unit of measurement the length of a horse's neck; one-quarter of a horse length.

Nose: The smallest advantage by which a horse can win.

Objection: A complaint filed by a jockey, trainer, or owner after a race against another horse or its rider.

Official: The designation given to the order of finish of a race in terms of payoffs to bettors by the stewards.

OTB: An acronym for off-track betting; a place not at a racetrack where a wager can be placed and tickets cashed and simulcasts are played on projection screens of the actual races being run at various racetracks.

Overweight: The pounds that a horse carries in the race in excess of its assigned weight because the jockey is too heavy.

Owner: The name of the person who owns the horse and whose name appears on the back of the foal certificate. Also the name of the person who currently owns and has paid for the horse if different from the name on the original foal certificate.

Paddock: The area of the racetrack where the horses are saddled and viewed before a race. It is adjacent to the jockey's quarters.

Pedigree: Parentage or lineage; the genealogical record.

Poles: The markers around the racetrack that indicate the distance to the finish line.

Pony horse: Usually an Appaloosa or quarter horse, not a pony, that helps steady young, inexperienced racehorses.

Post: The standing point for the race at the starting gate.

Post parade: The period before the start of a race when the horses come onto the racetrack, walk in front of the stands, and then jog to the starting gate.

Post position: The position for a horse in the starting gate numbered from the inside rail outward, which is decided by a drawing at the close of entries before the race.

Preakness: The second race in the Triple Crown series for three-year-old horses run two weeks after the Kentucky Derby (approximately mid-May) at Pimlico Racetrack.

Purse: The prize monies offered in a horse race. It is generally made up of added money based on the handle (total amount wagered) and sponsors' contributions and nomination, sustaining, or entry fees.

Racing Board or Racing Commission: A state-appointed body of people who regulate and supervise the conduct of racing.

Racing meets: The period of racing, usually in two to three month intervals, at a racetrack.

Rate: To control the horse's speed.

Receiving barn: The barn for horses that are shipped in to a racetrack.

Ridden out: When a horse wins a race without the rider urging it to its utmost because it is far ahead of the second-place horse.

Scratch: The withdrawal of an entered horse from a race after the closing of entries for that race.

Sex allowance: A reduction of three to five pounds in the weight carried by fillies and mares when racing against male horses.

Shedrow: At the track barn, the aisle in front of the stalls in which the horses are kept.

Silks: A jockey's racing shirt and cap displaying the owner's identifying colors.

Sire: A male parent of a horse.

Sprinter: A horse that can run fast for six furlongs or less.

Stakes: A horse race with entry fees paid from the horses' previous earnings. A horse that runs in stakes races is usually better than the average allowance horse.

Stallion: An uncastrated male horse that can be used to breed mares.

Starter (horse): A horse that left the starting gate when the door opened. A horse is not considered a starter if the door did not open because of mechanical failure.

Starter (person): The official in charge of starting the race who supervises the gate crew.

Steward: The racetrack official who presides over the race meeting.

Stick: The jockey's whip.

Thoroughbred: The name of a registered breed of horse. A horse bred from pure bloodlines not mixed with those of other breeds.

Triple Crown races: A series of stakes races for three-year-old horses that begins with the Kentucky Derby run at Churchill Downs in Louisville, Kentucky, the first Saturday in May followed by the Preakness run at Pimlico Racetrack in Baltimore, Maryland, two weeks later and by the Belmont Stakes run at Belmont Park in mid-June. A horse becomes a Triple Crown winner if it wins all three races, a feat achieved by only eleven horses in the 125 years of the series.

Turf: The infield grass racecourse on which some races are run.

Two year old: A Thoroughbred horse on or after January 1 of the second year after the year it was foaled.

Valet: An employee who takes care of the jockey's equipment.

Veterinarian: A medical doctor who treats animals.

Winner's circle: The part of the racetrack where the winning horse, jockey, trainer, and owners stand to receive awards and be photographed when their horse wins a race.

Wire: The finish line.

Work: The timed tryout on the racetrack that gives an estimate of the horse's ability to run and to win a race.

Yearling: A one-year-old horse; a Thoroughbred horse on or after January 1 of the first year after the year it was foaled.